NEW CANAAN
1950 – 2000

1951: The high school band crosses South Avenue at the head of the parade marking New Canaan's 150th anniversary

NEW CANAAN

TEXTURE OF A COMMUNITY
1950 – 2000

David H. Finnie
Editor

A Publication of The New Canaan Historical Society
New Canaan, Connecticut
2001

The title page drawing of Philip Johnson's glass house is from a 1979 NCHS invitation

Copyright © 2001
The New Canaan Historical Society
All rights reserved under International
and Pan-American Copyright Conventions
ISBN # 0-939958-04-X
Printed in the United States by
Colahan Saunders Corporation
First Edition

Dedicated to the Memory of

Mary Louise King
(1911 – 1996)

A native of New Canaan
who brought a new standard of professionalism,
historical insight and dedication to the study and presentation
of the history of the town she knew and loved

New Canaan Historical Society Mission Statement

The following mission statement, part of which appears in the 1889 constitution of the New Canaan Historical Society, was revised and expanded by vote of the Board of Governors in 1978 and is frequently revisited by the Governors.

The objectives of the founding members of the New Canaan Historical Society were *to bring together and arrange the historical events of the town of New Canaan, the genealogies of the families who have lived in town . . . to form a library and to collect relics and curiosities, to form a museum.*

Our mission now places research and education as the Society's primary functions. The Society will realize its mission through historical and genealogical research into the history of New Canaan, the operation of a research library, the publication of books and pamphlets, exhibits, and education programs.

In Appreciation

Stuart Higley has been a catalyst in numerous ways in New Canaan organizations: a founder of the Presbyterian Church; initiator of the steering committee and first president of the New Canaan Fund, Inc. later the United Way; the spark behind and first President of the Board of Realtors; member of the first board of the New Canaan Land Trust, Inc; vice-president of the first board of the Nature Center; author of several books, including Nature's Other Universe. *Our thanks to Stuart for his great interest in the history of New Canaan and for the concept of this book.*

New Canaan has deep roots previously documented in *Readings in New Canaan History* published in 1949 and *Portrait of New Canaan* published in 1981. This book is a continuation of the publishing tradition of the Society. It is not meant to be a definitive history, but a broad overview of the fifty years since 1950 by authors well versed in the rich heritage of New Canaan. Space limitations have made it impossible to include all organizations and many traditions well known to residents.

The inspiration for this book came from Stuart Higley who encouraged both the director and the publication chairman of the Society to produce a new book in this bicentennial year. It was Stuart who met with the publications committee when approval for the book was sought. The committee chaired by Joseph Sweet with Marilyn O'Rourke, Betty Black and Ruth Carroll and the director in attendance voted unanimously for the project.

This publication was made possible by the generous gift of time, research and the knowledge of the contributing authors. A special thanks is due to David Finnie for his excellent editing and the laborious task of indexing. Dave was assisted by Jane Caulfield. I cannot express how dedicated they were to the task at hand and how beautifully they bound together the separate entities to form a unified story of the texture of New Canaan. Additionally, I wish to express my gratitude to our designers, The Casey Group, and partners Susan and Tom Casey who provided superb guidance, to Phebe Kirkham of the New Canaan Library for her research assistance, to the staff of the Historical Society for production help, to Joe Sweet for his assistance with photographs, and to the Governors of the Society for their support and enthusiasm for the project. The beautiful cover is provided through the generosity of Virginia Taylor. We are also indebted to Walter Richards for the use of his lithographs of New Canaan and to Syd Greenberg, John Bukovcik and Nina Bremer for the use of their photographs. The Society also wishes to thank Karl Chevrolet for their financial contribution which helped defray some of the cost of this publication.

— *Janet Lindstrom, Executive Director*

"Waveny Mansion" by Walter DuBois Richards

Contents

1 The Meaning of Texture 1
   The Editor

2 New Canaan, Now and Then 13
   Ed Chrostowski

3 On The Endangered List: New Canaan's Modern Houses 39
   Gwen North Reiss

4 Health and Community 43
   An Interview with Doctors Charlotte and David Brown

5 Nine to Five and Beyond: The Business Scene 55
   Joseph C. Sweet

6 Rosen's: A Slice of Old New Canaan 65
   Jane Caulfield

7 Town Restaurants Revisited 67
   Patricia Brooks

8 Schools of a Community 73
   with Betty Quinn and Hudson Stoddard

9 The Spiritual Dimension: The Churches As I Knew Them 83
   The Rev. T. Guthrie Speers, Jr.

10 Ice Storm in a Teacup 93
   E. T. P.

11 Youth Must Be Served: A Sports Commentary 97
   Don Souden

12 The Celebrated Case of John Senior, Junior 113
   The Editor

13 Writers: Our Flourishing Literary Scene 115
   Lester Brooks

14 Visual Artists: A Vivid Panorama 127
   Ann Bridgman with Ruth Carroll

15 A Bow to the Performing Arts 139

16 Related Historical Society Resources 141
   Janet Lindstrom

Index & Credits 143

Marshall Montgomery with his files

1 The Meaning of Texture

David H. Finnie

What does it mean to say that a community has "texture"? Plato's Athens must have had it; the same with Dickens's London and Emerson's Concord. Grover's Corners, New Hampshire, had the texture Thornton Wilder gave it in "Our Town." But what about an affluent American community in the outer suburbs of a major metropolitan area in the year 2001? What, if anything, makes New Canaan "special"?

Marshall Montgomery, a leading light of the Historical Society for many years, was a strolling encyclopedia of New Canaan lore, and he had answers to questions like that. He could buttonhole a newcomer and demand, "Do you appreciate that no other branch rail line in the world stops both at a graveyard [meaning Springdale cemetery] and a country club [Woodway]?" And if that proved to be a conversation-stopper, he could follow with many another. His lifelong avocation was creating personally a hand-written data base to include every soul who had lived here since Colonial times, a Sisyphean task as the population expanded and families moved in and out without telling him. When he said cheerily, "Meet you at the Room!" he was referring to the Historical Society's former rented space at the Library, now the Salant Room; he was disregarding the fact that the Society, in large part due to his own leadership and dedication, had long since moved to its own extensive campus, and by now had more rooms than it could count. An astute government bond trader by day, Monty loved New Canaan, and he lived it. He provided texture.

Our town has a wide array of community institutions, most of them organized locally at private initiative, that enrich the life of New Canaan and its residents. Most of them were started during the past half-century. They have thrived because there has never been a lack of people — Monty is just one of them — who care intensely about the town as the place where they live and hope to remain as long as Providence allows, and who work to make New Canaan a better place. For lack of a better expression, this is what we mean by "texture."

Here are a few editor's picks out of a hundred or more New Canaan institutions, in random order: Waveny Care Center; the Gridiron Club; the Community Foundation; the Historical Society; Strays and Others; New Canaan Inn; the Land Conservation Trust; the Outback (good luck to it!); the Library; the Y.M.C.A.; the Nature Center; our schools, both public and private; Senior Men's Club; Volunteer Ambulance Corps; Young Women's League; Silvermine Guild Arts Center; and Waveny Park (together with the Mansion, Carriage Barn, Powerhouse, Lapham Community Center, sports facilities and open land).

Since we can't deal with all of them, let's take one at random: the Gridiron Club of New Canaan. Its only discernible activity is an annual variety show — but what a show! Each year a committee gravely decides on a new "fall guy" (so far, always a male) who deserves to be raked over the coals and be rudely escorted into the Club's "Hall of Infamy." It is a riotous, albeit rather innocent, night out with a high-cholesterol dinner ("Please pass the butter and sour cream, but don't tell my wife!"); the performance is filmed and replayed on community TV. Although the Gridiron is still a male bastion, cheerfully tolerated by spouses as a "men's thing," women come to the dress rehearsals, and some are glad to help out with the production. (A few women have appeared on stage, but only as male characters.) The only qualification for membership is to have been there once as the guest of a member. The most important questions on the application form relate to what kind of work you would like to do when it comes to putting next year's show together.

But the boisterous camaraderie of the Gridiron Club has a deeper purpose. Under the guidelines of the selection committee, which consists of all living former fall guys, the candidate is chosen on the basis of what he has done for the town, outside of his own profession or daily occupation. The final selection, therefore, is in a sense self-perpetuating; it is a consensus of those who have already been recognized for their contribution to New Canaan's texture; their choice is someone else whose contribution has not yet been recognized, and who won't mind being razzed about it. Here is one participant's description of the process:

"We all arrive at the selection meeting with favorite candidates drawn from our individual professional and social exposures in town. The discussion — always very frank and off the record — provokes mostly loving laughter, but also some profound revelations about people who are 'taken for granted' in the community, though they have given generously to improve the quality of life in New Canaan. The choice ignores wealth, social position and personal charisma. The candidate gathers favor if his effort has been made quietly and without thought of personal gain beyond the satisfaction of doing what he does. It always comes as a surprise to the new fall guy when he is notified of his selection. It is a humbling honor."

And the fall guys have been a varied lot: three doctors, two barkeepers, a clergyman, high school dropouts, Wall Streeters, Town government officials, a cabinet-level statesman, about eight lawyers (oh, the lawyer jokes!), two editors, an educator, a publisher, local businessmen (but no big-time CEO's, of which the Town has had no shortage), a radio personality, and a commercial artist. Plus the irrepressible and inimitable impresario Paul Killiam, who produced the first show more than forty years ago and stayed with it until his death in 1998. Here are the names as they appear in this year's Gridiron program, plus a few words to identify each of them:

Paul Killiam on stage

1961   Carlton Hill, *Advertiser* editor; behind many civic projects

1962   Leslie B. Young, lawyer, Republican leader, chairman of Board of Finance

1963   Izzy Cohen, innkeeper and counselor to many a barfly; sponsor of town sports

1964   Robert L. Bliss, Republican leader, state senate; Gridiron co-founder

1965   Earl M. Smith, New Canaan Lumber Co., real estate developer; Waveny Care Center

1966   Stanley P. Mead, judge of Town Court, state senate; child and youth welfare

1967   Charles F. Kelley, first selectman; acquired Bliss property for Nature Center

1968   Julius Groher, star athlete in youth, lawyer, town commissions, raconteur

1969   Dr. Thomas P. Cody, surgeon for police and fire departments; Democratic politics

1970   Carlton S. Raymond, bank president, selectman, town commissions

1971   W. Riley Hogan, colorful caretaker of Mead Park tennis courts

1972   Jack Sterling, exuberant radio celebrity; local theatricals and fund-raisers

1973   Stanley R. Resor, lawyer, secretary of the army; other high government posts

1974   Chester Billings, Jr., Wall Street lawyer, astute long-term head of Planning & Zoning

1975   Roger B. Kelley, insurance agent, Democratic politics, local sports sponsor

1976   Paul Killiam, silent-film restorer, impresario, Gridiron founder and producer

1977   Charles P. Morton, tax assessor, first selectman, backed Schoolhouse Apartments, town historian

1978   Philip L.R. DuVal, magazine publisher, Old Faithful Antique Fire Engine Company

1979   Marshall Montgomery, see above

1980   Al Youmans, wonderful with children: juggler, Santa Claus, Easter Bunny

1981   Dr. Jerome Selinger, retired surgeon; key supporter of Historical Society

1982   Nick Lombardo, innkeeper, Town Players, sponsor of local sports

The Meaning of Texture

Gridiron Club 1982:
Front row (l to r): Dick Winfield, Arnold Stang, John Berg, Torch Lewis.
Second row (l to r): Ed Gutt, Lou Moreno, Bob Neilson.
Third row (l to r): Yorke Allen, Steve Stackpole, John Lowry, Jim Rogers, Bruce Cole, Tom Wright, Penfield Mead

1983 The Rev. T. Guthrie Speers, beloved Presbyterian minister; ecumenical social causes

1984 Hoyt Catlin, local business entrepreneur, Democratic politics

1985 Dr. David Brown, family physician, community health and problems of aging

1986 Edward L. Winpenny, stockbroker, outstanding racquet game player, Republican Town Committee

1987 Harry S. Noble, first selectman, Waveny Care Center supporter

1988 Yorke Allen, Town Council, state legislator, Schoolhouse Apartments

1989 John G. Matthews, town commissions, state senator, youth sports sponsor

1990 John W. Pickering, founder of Modern Plumbing and Heating, chief of fire company

1991 James G. Rogers, Jr., philanthropist with a notably lively wife, Henrietta, the town's first female selectman

1992 Curry E. Ford, vice-president at Union Carbide, Y.M.C.A., founder of Senior Men's Club, Historical Society

1993   Ralph Pereida, artist, Parks Commission, designer for local theatricals

1994   Edmund J. Chrostowski, *Advertiser* editor; voice behind many civic causes

1995   Harry Coleman, dean at Columbia University, Board of Education, Gridiron star (in drag)

1996   Joseph C. Sweet, IBM lawyer, town band, town historian

1997   Dana C. Ackerly, lawyer, Interfaith Council, Waveny Care Center, other charities

1998   Jim Schlumpf, IBM, police commissioner, Senior Men's Club liaison with schools

1999   Leo E. Karl, Jr., Karl Chevrolet; high school scholarship fund, other charities

2000   Dick Brinckerhoff, lawyer, town commissions, state legislature

2001   Tom Moorhead, lawyer, chair of Town Council, president of Gridiron

It will be noted, incidentally, that several of these gentlemen of texture are contributors to this book. The Gridiron Club awaits a formal chronicler. The late Paul Killiam's voluminous papers are at the Historical Society; Don Souden, author of "Youth Must Be Served" (see p. 97) is curator of the collection.

NEW CANAAN IN THE HEADLINES

Yes, but aren't we in danger of too much introspection? How can we know what impact, if any, our town has had on the outside world, of which it is most assuredly a part? In the early twentieth century a local boy named Anthony Comstock (1844 - 1915), who grew up to be an officious, self-appointed anti-vice crusader, made his way into the *Encyclopedia Britannica*, apparently the only New Canaan native ever to have achieved such eminence. "Comstockery" is now a dictionary word for his career choice. Since then we have provided a home for our fair share of diplomats, theatrical and television personalities, captains of industry, financial talking heads, famous architects, and artists and writers by the hundreds. We have been visited from time to time by world-class celebrities, including Jack Nicklaus, Duke Ellington, and the Archbishop of Canterbury. There are old-timers who insist that shortly after World War II the unmistakable figure of Winston Churchill was seen ambling along Ponus Ridge on a Sunday afternoon. Someone has suggested sardonically that if we are looking for important visitors we might try the entry register at Silver Hill Hospital.

We have thought of a more practical way to take the temperature of our town's newsworthiness over the last half-century: by combing *The New York Times Index*. These indispensable tomes, published annually by the paper whose slogan is "All the News That's Fit to Print," list articles published in the *Times* in which our town or its institutions are significant players. Obviously the listings cannot be completely comprehensive. For example, many New Canaan weddings have been written up in the *Times*, but none is listed under "New Canaan" in the Index. Only one local sports story has made it — about the DeMichele quadruplets, superstars at the High School in the late 1990s.

Even so, we counted 162 entries under "New Canaan" for the years 1950 through 2000. The high point was 1957, with 13, including several about the evolving controversy over four-acre zoning, which eventually reached the U.S. Supreme Court. (See "The Celebrated Case of John Senior, Junior," p. 113) The general

The DeMichele quadruplets at New Canaan High School. From the left: Jennie, basketball captain; Chrissie, lacrosse captain; Julie, soccer captain; Brian, ice hockey. From the New York Times, *Nov. 15, 1997, with the caption "Meet the Quad Squad."*

trend over the half-century has been toward more coverage rather than less. New Canaan has not exactly been dying on the vine, at least as far as the *Times* is concerned.

A third of the entries in the *Times* contain hard news about the Town itself: zoning, to be sure, as well as various other political issues; controversial development proposals and projects (from RCA to Avalon); gypsy moth devastation of dogwood trees (1983); the deer problem (1998), and so on. Descriptive but less newsworthy are a dozen articles about the town generally, including several surveys in the Sunday real estate section purporting to describe what it would be like to live here.

There are seven items about the railroad, although the *Times* missed the most disastrous of all our rail mishaps, the fatal collision of two trains at the Grove Street crossing on July 13, 1976. There are fourteen pieces about education and the schools, mostly of a positive nature, and only six about crime and law enforcement. Another handful are about the weather: the great flood of 1955; the drought of 1980 (when the news peg was Water Company vans cruising the streets with loudspeakers urging citizens to conserve); Hurricane Gloria in 1985. But New Canaan was not news during the memorable ice storm of 1973, although it became so when a movie was made about the storm in 1996. (See "Ice Storm in a Teacup," p. 93). The New Canaan Library has five entries, including accounts of its expansions in 1953 and 1978. There are four items that tell about journalism awards won by the *Advertiser* in the 1950s. Philip Johnson and his Glass House estate are well covered, culminating in the transfer of the property to the National Trust for Historic Preservation and proposals to open it to the public after Mr. Johnson's demise. The Historical Society, we note with modest pride, has 26, heavily weighted toward the many notable exhibits at the Society's Costume Museum.

There are several other entries too miscellaneous to categorize, though some provide a glimpse of texture. In 1966, under the headlines: "Town Is Aroused by Secret Police; Formation of Citizens Alert Corps in New Canaan Is Assailed by Residents; Called Gestapo Tactic," the *Times* reported that police chief Henry Keller had assembled an unnamed group of volunteers to report to him privately and anonymously on incidents of vandalism like stolen mailboxes. The

From the New York Times, *February 16, 1986*

Metro-North Quest: A Haven for Bridge

By WILLIAM H. BALDWIN

Roger Roth

CARD PLAYERS on Metro-North trains are a raffish bunch, not to be confused with your ordinary submissive, silent, resigned rider.

Mostly they stake out corner locations, where there are four or five facing seats. Mostly they call their game bridge. A grandmaster of the bridge table would recoil at what goes on — or might even lose his shirt.

The first problem is to devise a lapboard. In the old days, some of the players with elaborate home workshops constructed fancy folding lapboards with tiny brass hinges and carried them in their attaché cases.

But the man with the board on the morning train would have to take the board to the evening train, and often he was unable to make the same train as the other players in his game. Nowadays, the game is played on the back of an advertising poster.

The trick to removing one of the cardboard posters from the wall of a Metro-North car is to insert a key, any kind of key, between the bottom edge of the board and the frame holding the poster. Work the key until you can get your hand behind the poster, and billow it out, until the poster is free of its frame.

Now you have a lapboard for your bridge game.

Bridge on the 7:04 out of New Canaan is likely to be a boisterous conflict, which irritates travelers in nearby seats. It gets the adrenalin flowing among the players, too. In fact, nothing that can come up at the office can match the morning bridge game for elevating your blood pressure.

It's not really bridge, but a bastardized version called "goolie" (derived no doubt from goulash). You deal each player five cards at a time, then another five, and finally three. You never shuffle the cards. Huge hands result; slam bids are frequent; you don't play any contracts for less than game.

The objective, of course, is to show up your own partner for the fool that he is. "Didn't you catch my Roman Jump?" You will ask with more than a touch of scorn in your voice. That explains why you went down six tricks at three clubs when he passed your three-club bid, not realizing that what it meant was that you had both clubs and diamonds, and you should have been in diamonds instead of clubs, his diamonds being much better than his clubs. Things like that.

Why do we have to use advertising posters for makeshift card tables? Painful question. For years, until recently, conductors provided laminated boards — also bearing advertisements — plus a deck of cards to each foursome; the cost, 15 cents each, later 25 cents each, and by last fall, 35 cents each.

In bygone days, a nonplaying commuter from New Canaan protested to the Interstate Commerce Commission and various other government agencies that trainmen were unfairly saving seats for card players, in return for illegal payments. Fortunately, nothing came of the protest, and the practice continued for years. Until now.

For reasons unknown to deponent, the official lapboards have disappeared, and recourse must be had to the less satisfactory, more flexible posters.

Replacing the poster when your train reaches Grand Central is rather tricky, and the explanation would be tedious; but this must be done, or the bridge players would suffer even worse reputations than they have now. It is bad enough to have to settle up for 2,000 points down at 1/20th of a cent a point when most of the loss can be attributed to your stupid partner.

We cut for new partners every day. For years, I have been looking for a strong partner who can carry me to victory, but have failed to find anyone who can do the job. There's nothing wrong with *my* game. ∎

William H. Baldwin lives in New Canaan.

chief was deluged with protests. "I didn't know it would cause this much stir," he told the *Times*. His initiative apparently disappeared without a trace; at any rate the paper never mentioned it again.

In August 1978 First Selectman Harry Noble invited the entire Board of Finance to his home (rather than Town Hall) for its final meeting of the year at 8 p.m., the regularly scheduled time, to be preceded by dinner. When two members of the League of Women Voters showed up there at 8 o'clock to cover the meeting, they were nettled to discover the board still in the middle of the meal. They declined an offer of dessert and waited in the patio until the meeting could commence. "It's not what you call an ideal climate for a meeting," sniffed Virginia S. Tarika, president of the LWV. But it made the *Times*.

Just before Christmas, 1983, there was a satirical restaurant "review" by local resident Mary Ellen Johansen of a mythical soup kitchen in New Canaan, after the manner of Patricia Brooks and her colleagues at the *Times*. It was inspired by an insensitive comment from Reagan White House aide Ed Meese about feeding the poor. Two years later appeared Bill Baldwin's delightful account of card games on the commuter train to New York (see p. 9). In 1979 the *Times* reported that 157 of the town's 14,200 acres were owned and protected by the New Canaan Land Conservation Trust; by the end of the century that figure had risen to at least 282 acres.

~~~~~

What we present here does not purport to be a definitive history of New Canaan over the past fifty years; that won't be possible for some time to come. Mary Louise King's admirable town history ended with 1951. When her book was published in 1981 she wrote, "What happened in the next decades [since 1951] is too close in time to be put into proper perspective. The future will have to judge whether the changes were good or bad for the town."

Being wary of change seems to be part of human nature, and for some of us this may be more true than for others. In May 2001 several senior residents were invited to the Town's human services office in Vine Cottage to discuss changes in our community. The *Advertiser*,

The Meaning of Texture

which covered the meeting, quoted Susan Dunn, who has lived here since 1953. "The whole world has changed; it isn't just New Canaan," she said. "Wouldn't New Canaan look funny in today's world if it didn't change?" True enough. And if change is inevitable, as veteran editor Ed Chrostowski suggests in the piece that follows, then a town is probably better situated to accept and deal with it if the town has some texture.

"The Old Willow Tree at Mead Park"
by Walter DuBois Richards

Texture of a Community

A view of Cherry Street from atop St. Aloysius Church, about thirty years ago. Just beyond the corner of South Avenue is I.B. Woundy's electrical shop, torn down to make room for an Eliot Noyes-designed prototype service station for Mobil. In the distance (circle and top photo) is Hoyt's flower shop, which was in the way of Charlie Kelley's Cherry Street extension plan. The story is told on page 16.

2 Our Town, Now and Then

Ed Chrostowski

Ironically, it is change that always has been the one great constant in the history of the world's civilizations and, of course, New Canaan has not been spared. It's a phenomenon that some of us, at the risk of sounding like dinosaurs with a fixation on the past, lament. It's not at all that we are displeased by what is. It's just that we have a nostalgic yearning for what was.

Indeed, New Canaan once clung so desperately to its bucolic idyll that resistance to change became an obligation of "proper" community attitude. The village folk of the past must have experienced that disdain as New Canaan evolved from an agrarian economy into a manufacturing center of sorts, then a summertime refuge for city people and finally now into an enclave of manicured lawns and "trophy houses." An old-timer at a town meeting almost half a century ago put it succinctly. "I've lived here 40 years," he boasted, "and I've seen lots of changes. And, I'm proud to say, I fought against every damn one of them."

Longevity in town was in itself once a badge of honor, and protection of status quo was regarded as exemplary community service. People speaking at town meetings almost always prefaced their remarks by reporting how long they had lived in town, as though to establish credentials for a right to be heard and legitimacy for whatever they wanted to say. Anybody with less than 25 years of residency would invariably be shouted down—"Sit down! You're a carpetbagger!"

That this sort of New Canaan pedigree is no longer a qualification for speaking out on public affairs is in itself a subtle reflection of the kind of metamorphosis the town has undergone in the past couple of decades. Our roots are not as deep; our community identity is not as clear. Maybe we're not as immersed in local lore, and consequently we're less appreciative of what it took to get the community to where it is.

Programs of the New Canaan Historical Society are vital in this regard. By making us more aware of the past, they make us more appreciative stewards of the present and thus more attentive and, it is hoped, better prepared to meet the needs of the future.

People coming back to town after only brief absences are quick to notice dramatic change. But they see it mostly in physical terms, buildings and roads where there once were meadows and woods. The greater though more subtle change has been in the town's personality, its character. Many old-timers sense more pretentiousness, more ostentation, more self-absorption now. Of course, that's not indigenous to New Canaan. It seems to be the prevailing mood in all of modern society.

We're also far less parochial than we once were. Just three or four decades ago, New Canaan was pretty much self-contained. You could buy anything from a spool of thread to a farm tractor without leaving town. Anything anyone needed was available here. That made us kind of insular, almost isolationist, though it also did engender a great deal of community cohesiveness and civic pride.

Now, New Canaan residents are heavily involved in regional programs, businesses, cultural offerings, charities and entertainment. We take greater advantage of regional assets and we contribute more to the development and maintenance of those assets. Not too many years ago, Kip Finch, local attorney and generous supporter of the United Fund (forerunner of the United Way), announced that he no longer would contribute to the annual drive because money was being allocated to out-of-town agencies. That sentiment was not unique. So much for our zealous self-sufficiency.

As we finally have become more regionally conscious, however, we now also are developing a greater regional conscience, recognizing a responsibility to help ensure the well-being of regional assets that benefit us all. We are more cognizant, too, perhaps that crime, pollution, poverty, housing inadequacies, traffic bottlenecks and other regional problems do not stop at the town line. We were not always so socially aware.

Decades ago, however, we were indeed more isolated in our preoccupation with what was happening only here at home. The shift was gradual as the nature of our residential community began to take on a new look. No longer just neighborhoods of single family homes on wide expanses of lawn and woods, we began to accommodate "congregate living," condominiums and apartments that were largely unfamiliar to us until the 1970s. Many of the stately old Victorian houses that once lined Main Street and South Avenue so gracefully were razed, for this new housing. The magnificent Valentine estate at the corner of Bank Street and South Avenue, for example, gave way to a huge condominium complex, one of New Canaan's largest and finest. Hundreds of new apartments, since condominiumized, were erected along a new road, Heritage Hill, cutting through the woods and fields just off downtown Main Street. And there's a supermarket, Grand Union (now Shaw's), where kids once camped and, during World War II, tended "victory gardens." At the same time, "McMansions" began to fill the fields and woods where children once played, the state supreme court having cleared the way in the 1950s by ruling New Canaan's four-acre zoning valid.

A comment on the spread of condominiums. A Charles P. Miller cartoon from the Advertiser.

Traffic is now abundant and parking is scarce on the downtown streets that were tree-lined country lanes just two or three decades ago. Cherry Street offers perhaps the most dramatic case in point. Less than 30 years ago, it was a narrow little street without sidewalks. Trees on either side blended into a canopy overhead. (It has been said that the trees along Cherry Street were maples; the cherry trees were in Maple Street, a block south.) Cherry rose to a knoll that crested right about where the CVS driveway is now and then continued across South Avenue to Main Street, where it came to an abrupt halt at the front door of a white building that housed Hoyt's flower shop. There was a little fishpond out front and a couple of greenhouses stretched across the lots in back of the store, adding to the pastoral atmosphere that was part of the downtown scene.

The Costales-Kelley Pattern

Presiding over these changes, as though to ensure an orderly progression, was a series of first selectmen who, as native sons, were devoted to the small town atmosphere but farsighted enough to anticipate needed change and to prepare for what seemed to be seamless transition. Clarence E. Costales, first selectman through the 1940s and early 1950s, set a pattern for those who followed him in that office. His administration was notable for the admirable way it coped with the disastrous flood of 1955, when our rivers overflowed and claimed two lives, and for putting the unsightly Main Street and Elm Street power lines underground.

Charles F. Kelley, first to succeed Costales, served from 1957-1973 and recognized early on that there had to be a better way to handle the already growing volume of downtown traffic. He anticipated also that the business community soon would be needing a little more elbow room within its tight 77-acre zone. So, in about 1973, Kelley proposed construction of what he called "The Circle Route." His plan widened and flattened the existing two-block length of Cherry between Park and Main and then extended it right through the Hoyt flower shop and across the back lots. It was finally linked to what was then the lower section of Burtis Avenue, and then continued across East Avenue over what was known then as Baldwin Avenue, hardly more than a country lane, ending its arc at Locust Avenue. (It was a stretch, indeed, to call any of them "avenues.")

A few years earlier, the Town had widened a block of Main Street between East Avenue and Elm Street, demolishing in the process several old wooden buildings, including Cody's historic drugstore and Jake's Modern Barbershop.

New Canaan's Own Boulevard

But The Circle Route was perhaps the most ambitious road job ever undertaken by the Town. It required the removal of many trees, a circumstance that angered Lions Club members when Mr. Kelley, as guest speaker at the weekly luncheon in the old Melba Inn, outlined his plans. Edgar Clausen, a Smith Ridge resident, scolded Kelley about that. Wagging a finger, Clausen quoted Joyce Kilmer as he reminded the first selectman that "only God can make a tree." The first selectman drawled thoughtfully, "Well, that's not true. You can also buy them at the nursery."

A painting of the old Cody Drugstore by Charles Saxon

This exchange found its way into the columns of the *Advertiser* a couple of days later and Kelley was not amused. Even then, 25 years ago, he was politically correct and feared that his irreverent remark about the creation of trees had alienated the church-going and the tree-hugging vote. But he didn't want to risk alienating the hometown press with his anger and within minutes laughed and changed the subject to fishing. It was vintage Kelley at his best.

Those back lots at the foot of Burtis Avenue were mostly vacant, but there was a wooden building there that housed a World War II defense plant, Airdraulics, which manufactured components for the aircraft industry. Ray Fairty later used it for his machine shop. Burt Hanish operated his water treatments business in another big white barn nearby, but after The Circle Route came through, Brock Saxe opened a family restaurant, "The Carousel," there and a busy shopping center thrives on the site now. (New Canaan also had another defense industry during the early years of World War II; it was called Boots Aircraft and it began in what we know as "the telephone building" across from the New Canaan Library. Then it moved to Ponus Ridge where it remained briefly before relocating to Stamford. The company made nuts and bolts for aircraft manufacturers.)

Almost immediately, there were signs that Kelley was correct in anticipating increased commercial opportunity resulting from the new roadway. With recent construction of new office/retail buildings in the East-Cherry area, his predictions have been even more on target. And we can only speculate on how much worse traffic flow would be without The Circle Route. The whole area seemed so remote, so out of the way, then. Today, it's a busy hub of development.

OUR FADING FARMS

Development came at a price, however, if one is to consider the loss of more of our rural character. For example, there was a farm stand at the corner of Baldwin and Locust avenues. It was called "Four Seasons" and, if memory serves, it was operated by Mark Isselee. It was based in an old house there and the wooden stand outside offered fresh fruits and vegetables in season. There's a big brick office building there now, formerly occupied by the SCM Corpor-ation. A touch of New Canaan's agrarian past also lingered during the 1960s in Ponus Ridge where Kip Finch raised and sold turkeys on his estate, "Four Winds Farm," more as a hobby perhaps than a commercial enterprise. Most of his farm is now occupied by six "McMansions."

Oh, the loss of Four Seasons, only about 30 years ago, was not so traumatic. After all, we still had Vincent Fenick's farm up in Barnegat Road, where fresh-picked produce was always available, and Charlie Fairty's orchard in Old Stamford Road with the best corn, apples and cider in the state. In fact, the Fenicks also raised a few sheep at their place until some marauding dogs attacked the flock, prompting Vincent Fenick and his son Ed to pick up their shot-guns, much to the great consternation of police and neighbors. Alas, New Canaan by the mid-1970s had become too "citified" for Vincent, and he pulled up stakes, moving to "real" farm country in upstate New York.

Memories of those places make the recent public clamor for a Saturday morning summertime farmers' market (placed finally in the parking lot on the old Center School site at the corner of Maple Street and South Avenue) seem like just so much idle chatter. Until about 25 years ago, New Canaan still did have some genuine agrarian flavor. Mr. Scofield and some of his old cronies used to sit in the doorway of his Main Street furniture store and talk about it. They would stretch planks between the sills of the show windows to serve as benches where they sat and clucked their tongues philosophically at the passing world.

The tales they told were rich and poignant. An eavesdropper once heard Roswell ("Roz") Bryant explain that he always kept a cow or two on his property in Seminary Street so the commuters zipping past en route to the train station each morning could see a cow and wouldn't be lying when they bragged at their New York offices about living in "the country."

Roz was proud of his "critters." Charlie Morton once recalled that when he was tax assessor, Roz stormed into his office in the Town Hall to complain about the assessment on his prize heifer. Morton had set too low a value on it, Roz declared, his feelings hurt that the true worth of the calf had not been recognized. It was the only time in his long career, Charlie once said, that somebody had complained about his tax being too low.

That "Doorway Forum" at Scofield's reacted to all of the community news and had solutions for most of our problems. They chuckled when newcomers talked about preserving the town's "rural character." "Shucks, that's long gone," they'd say. As though to prove their point, they noted a report in the newspaper about Mike Saaf's rooster up in Frogtown Road. It seems that a young couple had just moved out from the city in search of country life in New Canaan and then cried "foul" (or was it fowl?), complaining to the Town Planning and Zoning Commission about that blankety-blank rooster crowing too early, too often and too loud, waking them before daybreak each morning.

Kelley in the Vanguard

Back to Kelley. Charlie was a consummate politician in the very best sense of the word. He had an uncanny knack for anticipating needs well before there was any indication of them. He had an understanding of what had to be done and the wisdom and willingness to do it. His determination was contagious, mustering the kind of public support essential to successful completion of projects that, he was convinced, would benefit New Canaan. It was the kind of leadership that made New Canaan great, the kind that led the community to so many good things—the Nature Center, acquisition of Waveny Park and the Bristow Bird Sanctuary, to mention only a few of the projects that marked his 16 years in office, each worth a story in its own right.

Long before ecology and environmental protection were buzzwords, Kelley spoke of the threats of air and ground pollution. Our first reaction was one of disbelief. Air pollution in the rarefied atmosphere of bucolic New Canaan! Surely, we thought, the first selectman was hallucinating. It was the kind of reaction that concerned Kelley. He worried about whether the public would answer his call for an "unglamorous" project. Schools and parks were easy, he mused, but garbage? Maybe not. He was determined and persuasive, however, and New Canaan built the cleanest, most efficient garbage incinerator in New England, maybe in the country. We learned to call it a "volume reduction plant" because it was so much more elegant than an incinerator. It attracted municipal engineers from as far away as Japan on inspection tours. Fred Mazzella, the plant superintendent, would become furious if and when anybody said that stacks there emitted smoke. Those puffy white clouds were steam, pure as the driven snow, he insisted.

Then the State shut down municipal incinerators and landfill operations in the name of environmental protection and the recycling of waste materials. It was probably for the best, but another bit of self-determination and self-reliance, something New Canaan always had handled so well, had been chipped away.

Revamping Government

Kelley was quick to recognize trends in civic affairs. He was very much aware, and not a bit pleased, that a town meeting was vulnerable to packing by groups with a special interest in whatever issue was at stake. Yet, the town meeting was cherished as a bit of pure democracy, and he was reluctant to let it fade from the local scene. He recognized, however, that the town meeting lacked the continuity and accountability essential to sound government because it formed and reformed with each session, constituted differently each time according to what was on the agenda.

To remedy that, in 1961, Kelley appointed a charter revision commission charged with devising a replacement for the town meeting. His defining moment must have come that spring evening when the Board of Finance was holding its annual budget hearing. A small group of local citizens lingered outside on the lawn, socializing as they waited for more people to show up. Suddenly, Kelley and Leslie B. Young, finance board member known as "Mr. Moderator" because he invariably presided at town meetings, emerged and informed the gathering that the meeting was over. The board had been waiting inside and when nobody came dispensed with the tiresome reading aloud of all the budget figures, approved it and adjourned.

Efficient though all that may have been, it was not Kelley's idea of a "government by the people." Even in the era of well-attended town meetings, he would "adjourn to the voting machines" whenever he thought there was a hot issue that needed to be decided by more than just those few people in the town hall auditorium. The referenda that we knew so frequently in those days were thus actually extensions of town meetings, Part II, as it were.

Kelley steered the charter revision commission to what we know now as a town council, constituted creatively enough for more responsible handling of legislative matters and yet retaining the basic functions of the traditional New England town meeting. Now the public vote comes when citizens petition for a referendum in reaction to a decision by the Town Council, and the debate rages while signatures are being gathered on those petitions.

There was a dress code in the 1950s: standing room only at a town meeting in the high school auditorium.

And referenda, all hotly contested, abounded. Even the conversion to a town council government was subjected to one. There also were proposals to move the train station to Fairty orchard (defeated twice), to fluoridate the public water supply (approved), to join the Southwest Regional Planning Agency or SWRPA (approved), to spray the town from airplanes to kill the gypsy moths that were devouring our trees (rejected) and to build a new high school (rejected the first time and then passed at a second referendum).

The high school vote was especially interesting. The first one was held on the day before Christmas and when the results were announced, defeating the bond issue proposal, Norman P. Ross, then chairman of the Board of Education, solemnly intoned, "There'll be no Santa Claus for New Canaan children this year." However, a new building committee, headed by Ted Hobbs and George Haynes, was appointed by Kelley, plans were revised, costs were trimmed and the project gained overwhelming approval in a second referendum.

It was typical of Kelley to allow what he termed "the public interest" to override his own personal philosophy. A case in point was the appointment of the town's first full-time professional director of public recreation, Jim Rosenberg. Kelley was reluctant to do it, explaining that once you have a director, he has to develop something to direct and that can be costly. But he felt the kids in town needed more supervised recreational opportunities than could be provided by Hans Schneider at summer playgrounds or Joe Coletto in the winter basketball leagues. Now, there's a staff of at least five, a suite of offices and hundreds of kids and adults participating in the recreation programs year-around.

1971: inspecting construction at the new high school. From the left: Charles Morton, George Haynes, Ed Chrostowski and First Selectman Charles Kelley.

Wonderful Waveny

Kelley was more responsible than any other single individual for Town acquisition of wonderful Waveny Park. First, Mrs. Ruth Lapham Lloyd gave 12 acres for a site for Waveny Care Center, then 40 more

Santa joins the seasonal fun at Kiwanis Park

for a new high school and then the remainder, more than 150 acres and the buildings on them, to the Town, except for the "castle" and the 50 acres immediately around it. Those she sold to the Town for a million dollars, which she then promptly gave to the New Canaan Library for its major expansion.

The night the Waveny deal was sealed—after a referendum, of course—was one to remember. It was time to celebrate, and a block party was held in the Morse Court parking lot. It seemed like everybody in town was there, and Dick Palmer, excavating contractor, stopped by on the way home from work and, still wearing his work boots, danced with Mrs. Lloyd as the high school band played rock-and-roll.

It was a fun time in New Canaan. Led by Ed Rabe, Jack Bach, Ralph Pereida and Dick Ahearn, the men of the Exchange Club held an annual "Father Goose Fair" to raise money for improvements at Kiwanis Park. The club also brought Santa Claus, aka Al Youmans, into Kiwanis Park by helicopter each December as school choirs sang carols, officially opening Christmas Village. (There was a time, 40 years ago, when the Exchange Club sold its Christmas trees in a vacant lot near the Town Hall; there's a condominium complex there now.)

Today, safety considerations would rule out tiny Kiwanis Park for a helicopter landing. But 25 years ago, when the park was rimmed by more open space than is the case today, even the annual Fourth of July fireworks skyrocketed there, courtesy of the American Legion, led by Lawrence "Lonnie" Wood.

Partisan Politics Takes a Back Seat

Kelley was a staunch Republican who had held federal and state political appointments before returning to his native New Canaan to serve as first selectman. But he was largely non-partisan in local civic affairs and formed a productive leadership tandem with Julius Groher, the Democrat who always ran against Kelley for first selectman. Far from being political rivals, however, each enjoyed the other's respect and together they were a great team. One year, at a candidates' forum sponsored by the League of Women Voters during a town election campaign, Kelley and Groher actually endorsed each other.

That kind of non-partisanship was also evident elsewhere during the Kelley years. Democrats served as chairmen of key boards, Margaret Becker and Hudson Stoddard on the Board of Education and Joe Toppin on the Park and Recreation Commission, for example.

In the era before home rule was passed into law, almost every municipal action had to be authorized by legislation in Hartford. These "special bills" made Tom "Doc" Cody, the Democratic chairman, the most politically powerful man in heavily Republican New Canaan, Kelley once observed. He explained that the state government in those years was controlled by the Democratic party and nothing would move through the legislature without a green light from the party chairman in the affected town. Thus, the governor and the legislature got the word from Cody who got the word from Kelley. In addition to being good friends, Kelley and Cody came to be allies in New Canaan's behalf.

Kelley, of course, would always win the race for first selectman, but Groher, with the third highest number of votes among four candidates for the three seats on the Board of Selectmen, would be elected to the board. In their mutual endorsements, these two political "rivals" knew full well what the outcome would be. One year, how-ever, Henrietta Rogers edged out Groher for that minority party seat on the board. Kelley reacted by immediately appointing Groher to the Board of Finance, a key post. Mrs. Rogers then became an excellent, influential selectman, perhaps playing the "loyal opposition" role of a minority party member more enthusiastically than Groher ever did.

IN HARTFORD'S HOPPER

There was a time, 30 to 40 years ago, when New Canaan wielded state and county power far out of proportion to its population, though certainly commensurate with its contributions to the political warchests.

Until the state amended its constitution in 1965, each town and city had two members in the House of Representatives. Molly Cunningham and Dick Brinckerhoff, both Republicans, were our two representatives and a town resident, Walter Mansfield and Bob Bliss, to name just two—often served simultaneously in the Senate, and New Canaan would have three resident legislators in Hartford.

With the change, municipalities were reduced to just one representative each. Reapportionment soon afterwards divided New Canaan into separate senate and house districts, combining them with parts of neighboring towns. Thus, there are now two senators and two representatives, none of whom lives in New Canaan, representing various sections of town. John G. Matthews in the Senate and Yorke Allen and, later, Leslie T. Young (son of "Mr. Moderator") in the House were New Canaan's last resident legislators. Local control already had been eroded with the demise of county government in the late 1950s because parallel political organizations consequently faded away also. New Canaan's Marge Campbell and Bob Bliss had been among the county leaders who had great influence in Connecticut's GOP.

In 1961, the State set up a new Circuit Court system, replacing the old town courts and diluting still another bit of local autonomy. Until then, each town had two judges and a prosecutor. It was a time when Julius Groher, Dana Hawthorne, Dick Brinckerhoff and other local attorneys were appointed by governors to dispense justice with a local flavor. The system, political but practical, was steeped in local lore.

Noble and the Gadflies

When Kelley finally decided to retire in 1973, Henry S. Noble, then GOP town chairman, stepped up to succeed him and began a six-year tenure as first selectman during what might be called the "era of the gadfly." It was a time of tight municipal budgets, and the New Canaan Taxpayers Association was formed as a self-appointed monitor of town spending. Almost annually, referenda were called to overturn budgets approved by the Town Council and they succeeded a couple of times, compelling officials to trim expenditures.

Led by Dan Provost, Anne Stone, Herb Tilley, Bob Caulfield and Vincent Fenick, the Taxpayers Association effort was directed chiefly at the school system, which was reporting decreased enrollments, but demanding increased budgets. One year, the "budget watchdogs" even filed an independent slate of candidates for the Town Council. Their election bid failed. There were other "citizen votes" during the Noble years. It took two referenda before the Town was able to buy property in Locust Avenue for a parking lot. The property had been the site of tenements owned by the Bucciarelli family, and Dave Mitchell had acquired it, torn down the buildings which by then had become New Canaan's only slum and proposed to build a shopping mall on the land. When he dropped the idea, the Town moved toward purchase.

Other significant developments began to take shape during the Noble administration. A hotly contested plan was launched to move the police station out of the basement of Town Hall and into a vacant building, formerly the high school, on South Avenue. Nine-teen more units were added to the Town Housing Authority's complex of subsidized apartments in Millport Avenue, and plans were launched to raze the outmoded Center School building, reducing the number of elementary schools here from four to three, where it remains.

In 1979, when Noble announced he would not stand for re-election, the Republican Party put up Charles P. Morton, a popular figure who had only recently retired as town tax assessor. He had also served on zoning and finance boards.

Morton's decade in office was marked by significant accomplish-ments, carrying to completion some of the projects Noble had launched or proposed and adding many of his own. There also was the inevitable tumult. After a bitterly contested campaign, a referendum approved more than a million dollars to renovate the vacant old high school building and move the police station there. New dimensions were added to the community's cultural attractions as Morton negotiated long-term leases for conversion of the one-time powerhouse on the Waveny estate into a theater for use by the Town Players. And what once was the estate's carriage barn became a gallery and recital hall for the New Canaan Society for the Arts. The Center School tract was converted into a park-like public parking lot, though again not without some controversy. With Bob Bliss, State Representative Yorke Allen and Terry Cooke, a housing professional, providing the impetus, the former junior high school building was converted into living quarters for the elderly. The Schoolhouse Apartments were

Charles P. Miller's cartoon comments on the town's parking problem

(right) Parking plan for the business district, from the Town's Annual Report, 1985

Our Town, Now and Then

At regular pre-dawn meetings over coffee and donuts, Bliss and Cooke briefed the *Advertiser* editor on the scope of the project and progress, or lack thereof, and together they planned strategies to inform the public and gain support. It took seven years and several Morton trips to Washington. The old school building then housed the offices of the Board of Education and a day care center. It was necessary first to show that the building was under-utilized, that there was need for housing for the elderly and handicapped, that the day care center could stay put and that new quarters could be found for the Board of Education.

The challenge was compounded by the federal Housing and Urban Development Agency policy against mixed uses in its subsidized buildings. Ever persuasive, Morton succeeded in his missions to Washington, convincing HUD that the elderly and the preschoolers could co-exist with mutual benefit. The building was converted into 40 studio apartments, and the basement quarters of the day care

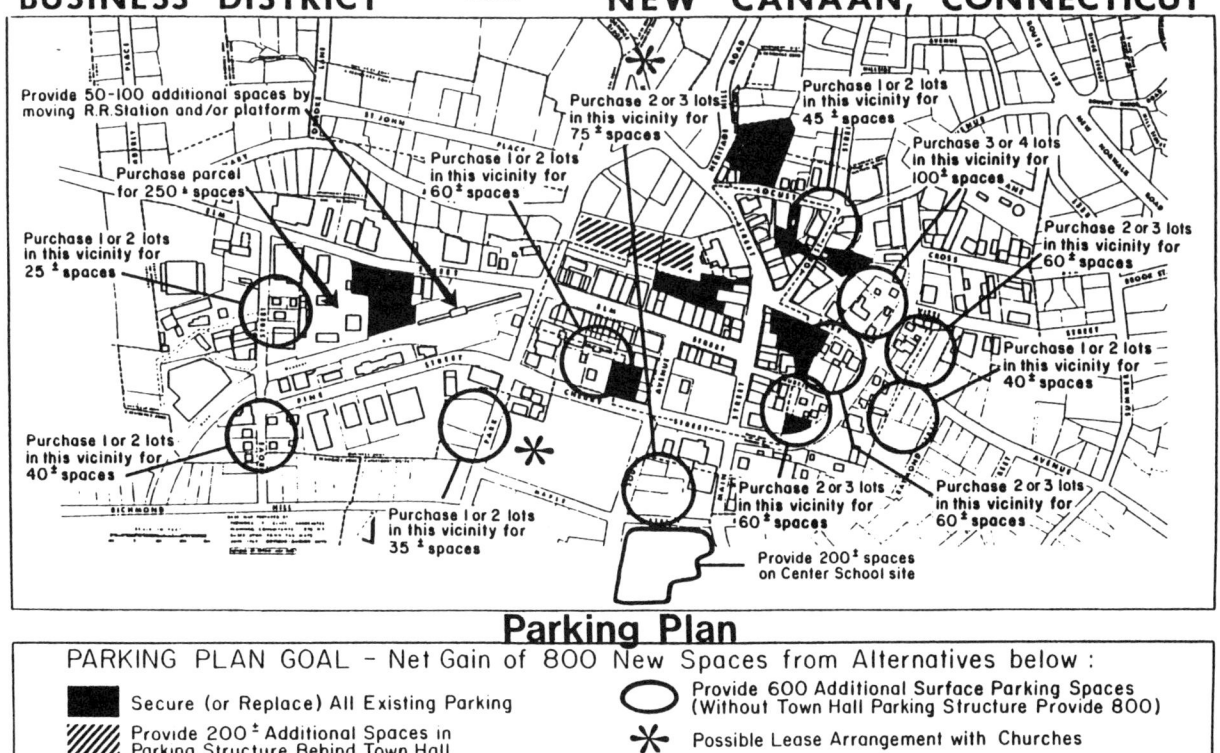

center were completely renovated under the leadership of Sarah DeCew and George Delage. As a consequence, HUD changed its policy nationwide.

Bob Bliss, Carina Milligan and a handful of others led the community effort that produced Canaan Parish, a development of 64 subsidized apartments for families. The project spanned the Noble-Morton administrations, but finally the complex was hailed as "one of most prestigious on the East Coast" because Town, State and Federal agencies had joined with the private sector in building it. The Town leased the land to New Canaan Neighborhoods, Inc., a private non-profit organization, for 99 years at a dollar a year, the State Housing and Finance Agency granted a mortgage loan and HUD subsidized the rents.

Morton's political philosophy was based largely on a minimal role for government and maximum participation by citizen volunteers. It was that spirit that led in 1979 to what is now one of New Canaan's most cherished community traditions, the Family Fourth Independence Day celebration in Waveny Park for which all funds had always been raised by bottle and can drives, sidewalk solicitations and door-to-door canvassing of local businesses. Today, the Family Fourth is financed largely by parking fees at the park, more efficient and easier, to be sure, but only at the loss of another bit of cooperative community enterprise.

Despite the Morton philosophy, as new requirements were imposed by Hartford and Washington and as new needs arose in society, the scope of town government ironically increased. For the first time, inland wetlands and conservation commissions had official standing and a summertime Youth Conservation Corps was established with a dual role, giving teenagers summer jobs and sprucing up town parks.

THE BIG LAND BATTLES

What were perhaps the greatest civic battles of the era were waged on the zoning front, however. When builder Harold Glazer proposed "cluster housing" on land off East Avenue, the Town Planning and Zoning Commission remained rigidly opposed, and he was forced instead to develop separate housing lots, though zoning did permit him to build a two-family house on each. When the neighborhood known as East Hills Drive was completed, the Zoning Commission was less than satisfied with the result and let down the barriers against condominiums and apartment buildings. In only a short time, the rush was on. It continues today.

The era also saw the end of the Hoyt's Nursery operations off route 123. Once touted as the largest nursery in New England, the 250-acre tract was acquired in 1970 by the RCA Corporation which proposed to build its headquarters there. Skeptics theorized that RCA was using that announcement only for leverage in negotiating new rental terms for its Rockefeller Center site in New York City. Others said RCA was interested in New Canaan only because its chairman, Robert Sarnoff, lived in nearby Westport. Whatever the reason, the Zoning Commission remained adamantly against a commercial use in a residential zone and, after months of heated debate in the community, RCA dropped the idea.

The Howmart Corporation, real estate arm of Sears Roebuck, acquired an option to buy the land and proposed a regional shopping center there. Howmart executives flew in from Chicago to show the *Advertiser* editor their plans and even a scale model. It seemed obvious that they had in mind the kind of mall now located in Trumbull, and they were quickly discouraged by everybody in town. The D'Addario firm in Bridgeport bought the land and developed the prime residential neighborhood that exists there now. The community breathed a sigh of relief; thanks to zoning officials like Chester Billings, Gouverneur Nichols and Bill Hart, we had escaped an office complex, the airport that the State once proposed to build there and a shopping mall which, foes said, would have turned Route 123 into "another Route 7."

Morton fended off other threats of intrusion on New Canaan's residential character. There was, for example, the state's plan to build an armory on Jelliff Mill Road. And there was a lawsuit brought by the Suburban Action Institute, a national organization, in an attempt to create more housing opportunity by cracking New Canaan's large-lot zoning code, declaring it to be unconstitutionally exclusionary. The attempt failed.

Moreno Moves In

When Morton completed his decade in office, it was time for another native son, Lou Moreno, to take over. By a margin that could normally be considered comfortable, some 650 votes, but was perhaps the closest ever for a Republican, Moreno defeated Democrat Priscilla Rutherford and was elected to his first term. He subsequently cruised, sometimes unchallenged, to four more two-year terms. Moreno died after being elected in 1997 to his fifth term in office. Like Kelley, Noble and Morton before him, Moreno had grown up here and had served the town in other capacities before becoming first selectman.

As might be expected from a first selectman who had been public works director for 10 years, Moreno focused on road improvements, and a systematic repaving program gradually covered the whole town. He also established a youth commission in town government, acquired an additional acre for commuter parking in Talmadge Hill, launched the conversion of sidewalks in the business district to attractive brick walkways, brought the Schoolhouse Apartments project to completion in 1989 and kept a tight lid on municipal expenditures, satisfying the taxpayers' challenges while still providing for all essential programs.

School Budgets and Asbestos

Moreno's tenure was marked by one of the biggest referendum fights in years after state and federal environmental regulations required removal of all asbestos from the high school building. When cost estimates ranged as high as $20 million, critics rebelled. Some urged abandonment of the building, others suggested closing it for a year while the work was being done and still others urged the town to flatly defy the regulations.

But Moreno appointed Hamilton Herman, an engineer who had held executive positions in federal regulatory agencies, to head a committee to plan the project. The debate continued to rage, but a referendum finally approved funds for the work after the Herman committee whittled costs down to about $6 million. The job finally was done with minimal disruption. Ultimately, the work also included some remodeling of the building to bring it into compliance with the federal Americans with Disabilities Act.

This was also a time of turmoil within the school system. Amid protests that the system was not meeting state minimum requirements for special education programs, a charge pressed by a parents' group (headed by Bruce Montgomery), veteran Superintendent of Schools Bill French and Assistant Superintendent Steve Rubin retired. The new superintendent, John Fitzsimons, arrived in 1988 and was, as teachers' union president Tony Jordhamo put it, "confrontational." After three years, his contract was not renewed by the Board of Education. The board itself was split on various matters. The Republican majority failed to agree even on the chairmanship, which finally went to Democrat Gordon Elicker on a 5-4 vote. He was ousted a short time later in a town election that featured a GOP caucus fight for school board seats. With the arrival of Gary Richards to succeed Fitzsimons several years ago, school operations seem to have been smooth until last year's heated flap over redistricting that transferred some students at West School to South School.

ANSWERING THE CALLS FOR HELP

Perhaps the most dramatic change over the past few decades occurred in the Police Department. During the Kelley years (and before), every member of the force was a "local boy." Most also had been athletes at New Canaan High School. The Police Commission, led at various times by such stalwarts as "Doc" Cody, "Pete" Raymond, Tom Carroll and Dr. Harold Wilser, required every man on the force to be involved in at least one youth activity as coaches for Police Athletic League baseball and football teams, mentors for scout and church groups or advisors to YMCA clubs.

The Norman Rockwell image of a small town cop was typical of New Canaan. It was never more evident than one morning when Officer Mike Williams was directing traffic at the busy Park-Elm intersection. A woman in a convertible pulled up for a red light and sat there as the traffic signal ran its cycle — green, yellow, red — a couple of times. When she didn't move, Mike, a big guy, kind of gruff but really good-natured, sauntered over and asked, "What's the matter, lady? Don't we have any colors you like?" Bystanders laughed.

Today, the woman probably would have reported the officer as impudent, and SUV drivers in the gridlock line would be leaning on their horns. The traffic officer probably would have approached the driver with a summons book instead of a joke.

Murder and Mayhem

Oh, it's not that the Police Department was all fun and games. There were more than our share of tragic traffic accidents, particularly along that stretch of Route 123 (police called it "Beer Can Alley") that was traveled by the young seeking out the later hours and lower drinking age eligibility in places across the state line in New York.

There was the abduction of a nine-year-old girl from Kiwanis Park and the discovery of her body some days later, a mystery that remains unsolved after 30 years. In 1989, there was a police shoot-out at Talmadge Hill and Old Stamford Road with a carful of men from the Bronx fleeing a drive-by shooting in Stamford. All were apprehended; one wounded critically. No police officers were hurt. A decade ago, there was a murder in Rosebrook Road, solved with the arrest of two local men several days later, and in the early 1970s there was the slaying of four members of a Lakeview Avenue family in their home by a fifth member of that family, who fled, but was apprehended in Arkansas and brought to justice within a week.

Even the change of command in the Police Department was dramatic. About 30 years ago, the *Advertiser* editor was called to headquarters one Thursday morning by Commissioner Wilser who said he had an important announcement to make. His statement that Chief Keller was resigning was interrupted by the Chief's comment, "That's not true, Ed. I've been fired." And that's the way it was reported in the paper.

"Red" Keller, a native son and former athlete, was a popular chief, highly respected for his efforts to enhance professionalism in police work. He was instrumental in establishing a training academy in Meriden for municipal police from throughout Connecticut and, in fact, the auditorium there is named in his honor. But he also was headstrong and had a falling out with Town Hall. The news of his "dismissal" angered the community, and there was a campaign, including newspaper ads and public petitions, to have him reinstated. It was to no avail. He was succeeded in the post by another town native and veteran policeman, Deputy Chief Frederick P. Tiani, whose tenure was cut short by his illness and then his death. Ralph M. Scott, also a New Canaan native and a lieutenant in charge of the detective bureau, succeeded him and retired after 10 years.

The Police Commission then went outside of the Department for a new chief for the first time, hiring Erik Dam, a veteran professional law enforcement officer from Ohio. Chief Dam retired after a decade, and the Commission returned to the ranks for a new chief, appointing Capt. Christopher Lynch.

No Cause for Alarm

No reflection on small-town Americana would be complete without a bow to volunteer fire departments. Born of necessity and a spirit of neighborly aid in the country's earliest years, these departments progressed steadily from bucket-brigades and village men huddled over checkerboards to modern, well-trained, fully equipped firefighting forces. The New Canaan Fire Company No. 1 is one of those departments. Oh, men still gather at tables in the firehouse to play games (not checkers!), but a fleet of varied trucks and state-of-the art high-tech equipment have joined the axes and hoses in the arsenal of fire-fighting weapons.

There was a time, as recently as 15 years ago, when the firehouse was a hub of social life for the community's young men and there was a waiting list for membership. One had to be invited to join and then to clear the "black ball" voting system of the incumbents. Now, volunteers are hard to come by and the paid staff has grown in just 20 years from two to fourteen.

Nor has the fire department, revered as it is in an appreciative community, escaped its share of controversy in the past couple of decades. There was a bitter debate and referendum over an addition to the firehouse (should we expand it, relocate it or build a second station elsewhere?) in the early 1960s. Just a few years ago, as the paid staff began to grow, there was another fight over a proposal to appoint, for the first time, a paid chief. In an effort at compromise a "foreman" was hired to supervise the paid men, but after a year (1992), the plan went down in flames and the fireman who had been hired was dismissed. Now, the senior man on each shift supervises that shift.

New Canaan's other emergency service, the Volunteer Ambulance Corps, had relatively smooth going. Until 1975, the Police Department operated the Town ambulance, an old Cadillac garaged in the police facilities in the Town Hall basement. Calls for ambulance necessitated taking two police officers off patrol (sometimes that was the entire shift), and the town concluded that the system not only delayed ambulance response but sapped police presence. Police officers had only minimal training in emergency medicine until about 1970 when Lt. Chet Lewis and then Capt. Jim Corson took Norwalk Hospital's 76-hour course for emergency medical technicians. Other officers soon followed.

Then Phil Bliss and his wife Jeanne almost single-handedly organized a group of volunteers to answer ambulance calls, though a policeman still drove the vehicle at first. Training sessions, far more exhaustive than those earlier ones, were arranged and within a few years the corps got its own headquarters, though not without some controversy as it took over a Board of Education garage, making it necessary to build a new one for the school system. For a while, police officers continued to drive the ambulance on calls, but a trained volunteer also responded and then the Volunteer Corps took over the operation completely.

Now the corps has two fully equipped modern ambulances and a "first response fly-car," operated by a professional paramedic around the clock, seven days a week, under a contract with Norwalk Hospital. Ambulance service continues to be free to New Canaan residents, though another controversy may be in the works following recent suggestions, notably by First Selectman Richard P. Bond, that the corps should charge a fee and leave it to patients to recover their costs from their health insurance companies.

Enter Dick Bond

Bond was selected by the Republican Town Committee to serve the balance of Lou Moreno's term after Lou died. Subsequently, he was elected to two 2-year terms of his own and the record of accomplishment that highlighted the administrations of his predecessors—Kelley, Noble, Morton and Moreno—continues under Bond with fresh impetus. Under Bond, several pending community improvement projects were advanced or completed. Others, including a swimming pool and a teen center, are underway.

Bond did not escape the turmoil that marked the administrations of his predecessors. He presided, for example, over the Town's acquisition of Earl Smith's former lumberyard on Elm Street, in an exchange of properties with Avalon, a development company proposing to build 160 apartments. Land at Mill Pond, called a park by many, went to Avalon for apartments and the lumberyard went to the Town for railroad parking. After a rancorous debate, which has had lasting repercussions in the split it caused in the Democratic party, a referendum approved the swap.

ECHOES OF WAR

Through it all in this past half century, New Canaan suffered with the rest of the nation through wars in Korea and Vietnam, two places that most people here had never heard of until then. Neither matched the intense emotion that wracked the town during World War II when more than 1,000 New Canaan men and women were called into service and 36 were killed in action. Less than half that number were in uniform during the Korean conflict and the home front, without rationing or air raid drills, was not as deeply thrust into the national effort as it had been during the 1940s. Small wonder that the Korean conflict was often referred to as "the forgotten war." Nevertheless, although there were no local fatalities, 10 New Canaan men were wounded in battle and two others were taken prisoner.

Not until a decade ago was there any kind of public acknowledgment of those who served in the armed forces during the Korean War. Then, a Veterans of Foreign Wars effort, organized by Bob Batterson, compiled a complete roster and arranged for the installation of bronze plaques in the Town Hall listing all the names.

The Vietnam War drew far more attention here at home. Not as many New Canaan men went off to fight, though five were killed in battle, but the community was gripped in the same clash of consciences that divided much of the nation as "hawks" urged full support of an all-out war effort while "doves" argued that the risk of American lives could not be justified and the nation should withdraw its troops. There were candlelight "peace vigils" on God's Acre and hundreds of "doves" signed full-page newspaper advertisements urging peace.

Yet, as controversial as America's involvement in Vietnam was, there was a timely effort to remember the New Canaan men who participated. Through a community project led by Dave Cammerer, a bronze plaque was added to the Wayside Cross monument at the foot of God's Acre.

Still "The Next Station to Heaven"

Yes, there have been losses in the changes that we have experienced over the past couple of decades. The impromptu civic affairs forums we once enjoyed at Izzy Cohen's bar ("Pierre's") and around a pot-bellied stove in the backroom of Ed Janis's Elm Street haberdashery are gone. Chain stores have replaced many of the locally owned shops that once characterized our business center. No longer are our stores and offices staffed by local residents. The electricians, carpenters, the neighborhood mailman, the cop on the corner, landscapers and plumbers we once called upon for help are not likely to be town residents.

Pierre's restaurant on Elm Street, also known as "Izzy's Place"

New Canaan now experiences a population shift three times a day. As most residents leave town for their jobs every morning, tradesmen and clerks and others come from elsewhere to work here in our stores, banks and offices. And, then, as they leave at five o'clock still another group of non-residents arrives to take advantage of our array of fine restaurants. That New Canaan should offer cuisine in such quality and quantity is in itself an immense change. Thirty years ago, there were few places to dine and the town pretty much shut down right after the last commuter train pulled in.

Everybody wants to be here to live, to work, to eat. That's an encouraging affirmation of the wisdom of our investment in New Canaan as home. But this daily influx of non-residents, this ever-changing make-up of our daytime and evening in-town population, also deprives the community of some of the continuity it once knew, the kind of regular presence that breeds community awareness and fosters the curbside neighborliness and civic debates that once were among the delights of a stroll through town.

Yet there is now a fresh resurgence in our town's economic vitality. Shopping and dining are superior. Our resources and our vistas have been expanded. Our "newcomers" are highly educated, highly talented, highly motivated, highly paid. They set high standards for community quality, and our best efforts to achieve them will continue to preserve and promote all the good things about life in New Canaan.

Ed Chrostowski is a lifelong resident of the area, and his 52 years in community journalism include 35 as editor of the New Canaan Advertiser. He is now editor emeritus and continues to write, including a weekly column, and edit some copy for the paper.

TEXTURE OF A COMMUNITY

What's going on in...

... the town with more modern architecture per capita than just about any other place in the East

"It seems to me there are about seventy-nine hundred out of our eight thousand population

"That wish to hell that Harvard and the Modern Art Museum

"Had provided padded cells for their brilliant graduate architects

"Complete with air-conditioned junctions and cantilevered sundecks—

"Windowless, doorless, charmless and escapeproof...."

This interesting bit of verse is from a lengthy poem that first appeared in the New Canaan (Conn.) *Advertiser* of March 13, 1952. It was signed by one "Ogden-Nash Teeth," but every New Canaanite will tell you, in strictest confidence, that it was Stockbroker Lewis Mack who was Nashing his Teeth in anonymous meter.

The Bard of New Canaan was, of course, irked by the houses shown on these pages. To H&H readers, these houses are pretty familiar, and some of them are pretty famous houses at that. And so are their designers. As every reader of this magazine knows, New Canaan is the home of men like Marcel Breuer, Philip Johnson, Eliot Noyes, John Johansen, Landis Gores and others. They have made New Canaan a symbol of creativeness in modern American architecture.

But if the bard is anywhere near right, and all but 100 New Canaanites tend to burst into indignant verse every time they see a flat roof or a glass wall, that would be a pretty serious matter for a lot of modern architecture and a lot of modern architects in the US. To get to the bottom of this, H&H has tried to make a fair survey of the situation. (See p. 136.)

Their conclusion: Things are looking up for modern architecture. Obviously, New Canaan is no "Middletown" for how many US towns are more than 300 yrs. old, or feel as tradition-conscious as Williamsburg? And how many US towns act as "dormitory suburbs" for well-to-do businessmen and professionals, whose preferences (from neckties to politics) tend to be conservative?

The dice are loaded heavily against modernism in New Canaan. If, in spite of this, modern architecture is making headway there, modern architects (and builders of modern houses) can be pretty sure that glass in the gable end will soon raise no eyebrow, that glass can reach from floor to flat roof and gain the same acceptance as the columns of the Colonial two-story porch.

1-3 by Philip C. Johnson
4-6 by Marcel Breuer
7-10 by John MacLane Johansen
11 by Landis Gores
12 by Marcel Breuer and Eliot Noyes

3   On the Endangered List: New Canaan's Modern Houses

Gwen North Reiss

The Historical Society joined forces this year with the New York/Tri-State Chapter of DOCOMOMO to begin the first scholarly documentation of New Canaan's Modern houses. The recent loss of a few of the more significant houses has inspired a number of architectural historians, writers, preservationists and concerned New Canaanites to research and document as many of the houses as possible. DOCOMOMO, the Historical Society's partner on the survey, is an international group based in the Netherlands. The name is an acronym for Documentation and Conservation of Buildings, Neighborhoods, and Sites of the Modern Movement.

One goal of the study is to create a centralized historical record of the many architecturally significant Modern houses built here beginning in 1947. "One of the most frequent requests at the Society," says Executive Director Janet Lindstrom, "is for information on the homes and architects involved in the Modern Movement. The documentation of these homes will allow scholars and writers to easily access an important part of New Canaan's history." Another goal is to provide detailed documentation to those who are in a position to help preserve the remaining houses. The recent economic boom has had the unfortunate downside of putting many of these houses at risk. Special attention paid by the architects to landscape and siting makes these properties all the more enticing to developers, who see them as easy teardowns.

First Selectman Richard Bond sees the loss of the significant Moderns as a reduction in the quality of the town. "The thing the town needs to do is to get the zoning board of appeals to allow variances so these houses could be expanded appropriately," says Bond. In what he sees as a parallel effort to the survey, architect Lew Bowman, who has served as a consultant to Bond on the subject of the Modern houses, has submitted suggestions for possible zoning incentives to Town Planner Hiram Peck.

(left) January 1953: early recognition of New Canaan as a center of Modern architecture. An eight page article from House and Home *magazine.*

Mary Donohue and John Herzan of the Connecticut State Historical Commission spoke to a group of enthusiastic volunteers at the Historical Society in January of 2001 to acquaint the group with the forms and criteria necessary for creating a historical record. The volunteer group includes architects, writers, historians, realtors and others with an interest in the Modern Movement. Led by Su Tamsett of DOCOMOMO and the Historical Society's Janet Lindstrom, the volunteers are in the process of researching more than 80 significant houses, including some that have already been demolished. According to Herzan, eight of New Canaan's Modern houses already appear on the State Register of Historic Places, with Philip Johnson's Glass House also on the National Registry. (Johnson donated his compound to the National Trust for Historic Preservation in 1986.) Of the eight houses, three were designed by Johnson and one by each of the following architects: Marcel Breuer, Eliot Noyes, John Johansen, Landis Gores and Frank Lloyd Wright. Though Wright never lived here, he designed one house in New Canaan; his protege, Allan Gelbin, designed two. The survey group may seek historic registry status for a few more of New Canaan's noteworthy residences.

Mid-2000: a cultural landmark falls

As readers of this book may know, architects Philip Johnson, Marcel Breuer, Landis Gores, John Johansen, Eliot Noyes and Victor Christ-Janer all settled in New Canaan by 1950. Breuer, Gores, Johansen, Johnson and Noyes, now locally known as the Harvard Five, came here from the Harvard Graduate School of Design. Christ-Janer studied architecture at Yale. These men and their younger associates, among them Richard Bergmann, Alan Goldberg, John Black Lee, Gary Lindstrom and Hugh Smallen, made New Canaan a magnet for magazine editors and architecture critics through the 1960s. Edward Durrell Stone also designed a house in New Canaan. Many of the houses built in New Canaan helped set the course of Modern residential architecture in the U. S. and remain icons of the era.

On the Endangered List: New Canaan's Modern Houses

During the 1970s and 1980s the houses were largely forgotten. Part of the problem for newcomers to the town has been a lack of awareness. "Now that the era has passed and new people are moving in, they don't even know what happened here," says architect Richard Bergmann, who has given grass-roots talks throughout the community.

New Canaan's Moderns have enjoyed a comeback recently in the design magazines, while preservationists are keeping an anxious eye on their fate. Locally, two small Modern house tours, organized by Richard and Sandra Bergmann and architect John Black Lee, took place in the fall of 2000. One of the tours was sponsored by DOCOMOMO, the other by the Antiquarians and Landmarks Society based in Hartford. Architect and furniture designer Jens Risom, who has lent his voice and presence to the preservation effort, spoke to the tour groups on the Modern aesthetic. Kathleen Randall of DOCOMOMO says her group came away from the tour feeling "we needed to do something to communicate the significance of these houses beyond our limited group and to try to do something as permanent and scholarly as the Modern Movement in New Canaan warrants."

Gwen North Reiss is a freelance writer who has written about modern houses for preservation magazines and for the DOCOMOMO international journal. She lives in New Canaan with her husband and two daughters.

1951: the Boy Scouts' witty float at the 150th anniversary parade displays the Philip Johnson Glass House on Ponus Ridge juxtaposed with Chief Ponus's tepee.

TEXTURE OF A COMMUNITY

TLC at the Waveny Care Center

New Canaan Inn: from left, Brent Bestercy, Stephen Stackpole, Betsy Gibson, Eve Jeffries

1981: Volunteer Ambulance Corps at the scene of an accident

4 Health and Community

A Conversation with Doctors Charlotte and David Brown

No one could dispute the designation of the Doctors Brown as New Canaan's pre-eminent medical couple of the last fifty years. From their eyrie on Garibaldi Lane they can survey a good part of the town to which they have devoted their professional careers. Dr. David was one of the founders of the New Canaan Medical Center on East Avenue, and Dr. Charlotte was the town's top public health official from 1956 until her retirement last year. Besides all that, it would be hard to name a good cause with which one or both of them has not been involved, from affordable senior housing to drug rehabilitation to the Waveny Care Center. In February 2001 they were gracious enough to welcome the Society for a joint interview:

Question: Our Bicentennial book will reflect many changes in New Canaan over the last fifty years. You hear people say, "My, how the town has changed since we moved here!" pointing to a new building going up. But there must also be a lot of continuity hiding behind the physical changes. How do you two feel about that?

Charlotte Brown: Something happened to us yesterday that bears out what you've just said. David and I went downtown to buy a Razor Scooter for me to use on a canal boat trip in Europe with some younger people who will be going off from the boat to see the sights, and I wanted to be able to keep up with them. [Charlotte has had her share of difficult knees]. Only weighs six pounds, put it over your shoulder and carry it. The owner of the toy store asked who is this for, and I said, it's for me and I explained why I needed it. Right away he shook his head. He said, "You can't have it; it's too dangerous. The roads around the canals in Europe are rough, they're very stony" and so on and so on. So we thanked him and left. He could have sold me a scooter, but he refused to, for my sake. There's still a good community feeling here.

David Brown: Although he didn't know us, it was obvious to him that we were old-timers, to be protected. He was looking past the profit; he was looking out for the welfare of his customers.

Q: Well that's a pretty good story, but what does it have to do with medicine?

DB: It has a great deal to do with medicine! People are healthier when they feel that they are part of a group that is regarded with special attention.

CB: It's important for public health that people in a community feel that kind of responsibility — which brings me to the difference between public health and private medicine. My job as a public health officer was protecting and improving the quality of life of the general public, rather than treating individuals. But sometimes it did involve specific individuals. About five years ago there was a New Canaan businessman who flew to London on the Concorde on Wednesday, flew back on Saturday, feeling very sick, went to the hospital on Sunday, and by Monday he was dead — of meningococcal meningitis, which is very contagious. I heard about this from the head of contagious diseases at Norwalk Hospital, and between us we had many phone calls with the Centers for Disease Control and also with the man's family. His wife was very cooperative, so very eager that it should not happen to anyone else — whereas someone else might have been mad, or too sad or upset to talk. The airline people were extremely helpful — especially the head stewardess — and said they would notify all the other passengers. I talked to the man's boss, so he could alert the people he had been doing business with in London. That was all part of my job, and in this case it certainly involved individuals.

Q: What was the practice of medicine in New Canaan like when you both arrived here in 1951?

CB: When we arrived there were four pediatricians, two surgeons, one eye doctor and one ENT man. They all had individual practices, though they covered for each other. A doctor could get x-rays, EKG's and certain laboratory tests — but had to rely much more on the patient's history and physical exam for diagnosis. There are so very many effective ways now of curing illnesses compared to fifty years ago — like organ transplants, cancer treatments, antibiotics and blood pressure management, to mention a few.

Paying the doctor in those days was strictly between the doctor and the patient. Hospital admissions and stays were entirely at the discretion of the physician. There were no HMOs to tell the doctor what he could do and when he could do it. As for public health — there really wasn't any in New Canaan. No inspection of restaurants, no supervision of wells and septic tanks. No follow-up of diseases, although the Connecticut state department of health kept its eye on the public water supply, and specialists from Yale did study the polio epidemic here in 1953.

Q: There was a pediatrician here named John Frothingham, wasn't there?

CB: John was a doctor who practiced the art of medicine. He had a wonderful way with children. John always traveled with his mongrel dog, a regular mutt, and the children loved that. He would tell them stories. He went one night to see a child whose parents had gone to New York. The baby-sitter had called the doctor because the child seemed sick. When he walked in, she walked out, because she was afraid. So John called his wife and said, "If you want me, I'm here baby sitting!" When the parents got home they saw the doctor's car in the driveway, and that gave them quite a start. But their child was sound asleep.

DB: I'll tell you another story about John. A mother called him and said, "My two-year old just took a bottle of my husband's heart pills." They were digoxin, which can be a little bit toxic in an adult, but a whole bottle would be fatal in a small child, no question about it. John said calmly, "Don't worry. Don't worry at all." But he raced over to the house, pumped the child out and saved a life. He felt consideration for the mother, who had a few moments of peace before he got there.

CB: Doctors these days make a big mistake not making house calls. Of course, it can be very time-consuming. Telling the mother to call 911 for an ambulance is often the best thing or the only practical thing to do. But going there gives a doctor an opportunity to see what conditions are like. You can see whether a mother is maybe neglecting her child. An old person may say she can cope, but she has to go up and down fifteen steps every time she does anything. Her house is cold, because she hasn't been able to pay the oil bill.

DB: Treating the disease came first of course, but often it was not the only thing a doctor on a house call had to do. I could find myself in the kitchen boiling up water for hot lemonade or tea, or fixing the furnace, or unplugging the toilet, or taking a fish hook out of an ear. You would sit down with a family and say, "Your Uncle Joe has had a stroke, and one of you has to be here all the time," and sit there while they worked out an arrangement. As my career went along, social service workers and physicians' aides came on the scene.

CB: We happen to have a social worker in New Canaan who is so good, so dedicated. She was brought up in New Canaan, a member of an old family in town, and she got a master's degree in social work. She wanted very much to work here, but the first selectman at the time didn't approve of social workers, so she applied for a job as a secretary in the social services department. But she dealt with the selectman in a nice way, and before long he thought the sun rose and fell on her, and he changed his mind completely about social workers.

David was called one night by a woman who had lots of money, lived in a nice house, but it was in terrible condition. She would only buy 40 gallons of oil at a time, and the house was cold because the oil company wouldn't deliver any more that way. After determining that there was nothing much wrong with her except she was cold, he offered to start a fire for her in the fireplace. He went to the cellar to find some firewood, which was all nicely stacked. When he came up she shrieked, "Not that wood!" He had to go down again and scrounge around for scrap lumber to light her fire. And did she say thank you? She did not!

Q: Sounds like she needed a social worker all right. Tell me more about being director of public health. How did you get the job?

CB: I got the job in 1956 because the Republican and the Democratic town committees asked me to do it. The incumbent had been there for many years. He did very little, because he felt very strongly that people did what they did because that was what they wanted to do. If you bought a house with a bad septic tank, or ate in a restaurant that was contaminated, that was your tough luck. Shortly before I took over, a man bought a house on Nubel Lane for $40,000, which was a lot of money in those days. It was in the middle of winter and the house looked very, very nice; it was in the woods;

there was this beautiful snow all over the ground. But when spring came and the ground thawed, the sewage bubbled out onto his driveway. It was just all over the place! He was from Washington D.C., and he told me, "Down there I never gave the toilet a thought after I flushed it." Needless to say, he was very distressed, and he thought he had been swindled. And he spent a whole lot of money scooping out his swamp. There were too many episodes like that, and it was decided that the town needed a director of health who would take some interest.

I talked to our old professor of public health, who was retired and living in Weston. "Well," he said, "if you take the job you won't actually have to remember too much of what we taught you in medical school. The most important thing is to get some good help in your office, a trained sanitarian if you can find one. Then you have to get on good terms with the local newspaper. Also call up the officials in Hartford, because Connecticut has the best state health department in the country. They will be very surprised when you introduce yourself and say you want to come up and see what they do."

Well, I did that, and they were absolutely overcome! Hartford sent down a sanitarian, because what was I to do? I didn't know anything about septic tanks! He came once a week for a while, and then he said one day, "I'm sorry, Dr. Brown, I can't come here every week forever. I have to take care of the whole state." So I talked to Clarence Costales, our first selectman then, who said, "OK, we'll get a sanitarian, but first we have to sell the idea to the Board of Finance." He showed me a list of the members of the Board of Finance, and being fairly new in town I knew only one of them and he was a Democrat. He was very supportive, but that was obviously not enough. So I said to myself, what the hell, I'll call up Les Young, the Republican party leader, whom I had barely met. He argued and argued with me about why we shouldn't have a sanitarian. Then about two o'clock the next morning Clarence called to tell me that the Board of Finance meeting had just broken up; they had been arguing into the night and had finally decided the town could afford a sanitarian. He said, "I want you to write a long, long letter of thanks to Leslie Young, because without him we wouldn't have got it." I thought that was very peculiar, because Les had argued so hard against it when I talked to him. So instead of writing a letter, I called him up for an explanation, and he said, "If I hadn't argued with you and heard your answers, I wouldn't have been able to answer the arguments at the Board of Finance." That day I learned a little about politics!

Our young son Rush used to come with me on my rounds after Center School let out. One day we went to visit a new housing development off South Avenue, right next to a swamp. (There was no environmental commission then). I flushed dye down the woman's toilet, then Rush and I went outside to trace the dye. A few days later Rush was admiring the colors in the feather duster our cleaning lady was using, and he wondered what birds the feathers might have come from. She told him they had probably been dyed, and asked if he knew what dye is. "Sure," he replied, "it's what my mother and I put in people's toilets and watch it come up in the yard!"

The sanitarian and I spent a lot of time checking on restaurants. The conditions in the cellar dining room of one of the fine old inns in town were dreadful — it was unbelievably filthy. And I remember one cafe-deli near the corner of Main and Elm. This guy had a warming table that operated on gas jets, and there were mountains of heaped-up grease. It was just luck that he didn't have a fire. It could have burned down the whole corner — all those old wooden buildings crowded together.

Q: How did you deal with something like that? Close them down? Take them to court?

CB: No, because they would generally agree to close temporarily while they cleaned it up. One Chinese restaurant shut down for a few days, and when we came back the staff were all lined up to greet us in immaculate white uniforms, with clean napkins folded over their arms.

At one of the private schools a few years ago they served lunch as usual one Tuesday, and the next day 85 children and most of the faculty didn't show up because they had been throwing up all night. We went out to see what was going on. They had served sandwiches on Tuesday made from turkey put out by the state Department of Agriculture. We tested what was left of the turkey, and it was fine. The bread was fine. We tested the mayonnaise and it was fine. We did throat cultures on the cook, which were negative. So this was a great puzzler. And then the cook confessed: on the previous Saturday her granddaughter had come to visit overnight and had thrown up, and on Monday the cook herself had thrown up all night. Although she was feeling terrible on Tuesday she came in anyhow, and spent the morning breathing on all these sandwiches while she put them together.

With something like that, I would call Hartford, and they helped out by paying for the tests, which otherwise would be quite expensive for the school or for the Town. They were very cooperative — every time.

Q: Did your practice as a pediatrician overlap with your official duties?

CB: It conflicted with my duties as a mother. I realized that I couldn't practice medicine and raise three children at the same time. I know some women do that, but I couldn't. I became director of public health when our youngest, Isabel, was two years old. Of course, it wasn't a full-time job. Sometimes a week would go by when I didn't do anything.

Q: David, you had a lot to do with the turnaround at the Visiting Nurse Association, didn't you?

DB: I had a great deal to do with the VNA, which was archaic by any standard or measure. In the summer of 1989 Jane Resor, the head of the nominating committee, came to see me. She looked me in the eye and said, "You've just retired, and we need someone to run this place." Jane wasn't used to taking no for an answer. Under that kind of duress I said I would. And they elected me president. I looked over the aging faces of the board, and I thought, well, we'll have to make some changes here. The record-keeping and the books were in terrible shape, and they were going down the tube financially. The staff were complaining about the regulations: "By the time we finish filling out papers, there isn't any time left to see patients." But they had a marvelous health insurance plan for themselves, about the best in the country, we discovered.

The recently appointed director of the VNA was already in hot water. She had used vulgarities in a speech to students about safe sex, and when queried about it she gave a profane response. All this, and a lot more, got in the *Advertiser*. Letters to the editor complained about "gutter-language," neglect of duty at the schools, denial of service to terminally ill patients, and general lack of compassionate care. One letter launched a petition to have her removed. An editorial declared that "the VNA at this point needs more than just funds," implying much the same thing.

So I said to her, "First of all, we've got to streamline our business operations and stop running up these deficits. Second, we've got to work on getting a good press again. And third, we need proper reports on all our cases, and I want to see our case load going up." I explained a few other points I had in mind and said, "All this will make perfect sense to an intelligent woman like you, but if I hear about any of these things not being done, we're going to have to talk about your retirement." She resigned that very day. We didn't even have to offer her a severance package.

As for the lavish benefit plans, we were told by experts that the only thing to do was buy them out. I wrote a lot of sweet letters to the people who had been doing the nursing, offering them a rather generous package to give up their benefits. So within a week I had the resignation of the director, and most of the staff had accepted the insurance buy-out.

CB: At that time I was also health director in Wilton, and I had seen what wonderful things were being done there by Joyce McConnell and her people at Nursing & Home Care. One day David and I were driving down along Route 7 into Wilton, and I said, why don't we stop and you can talk to Joyce.

DB: And it worked. At first, while we were working out a formal merger into NHC, we set up an interim arrangement whereby they provided direction, office support, and nurses as we needed them.

Q: How did you persuade your board that the VNA had to be merged?

DB: I hate meetings, because often just one person can turn a whole group. So I went around and talked to them all individually. And at the next meeting I said, "Six out of ten of you agree about buying out the health plans, and therefore that's what we're going to do. Most of you seem to agree that we ought to turn the operation over to Nursing & Home Care. Now, is there any objection?" And they all agreed.

CB: Except for one person. I was at that meeting, being on the board ex officio. This woman said, "I think we're doing this too quickly. We haven't had time to consider this thoroughly." Whereupon Ike Houston slowly stood up, and out of his pocket came this letter he had written to the board two years before, suggesting that the VNA join with Wilton. He said, "We have had this under consideration for two years." That was the turning point of the discussion.

DB: And the results of the new arrangements were dramatic. By the end of the year we had a multiple increase in our number of home calls, without substantial damage to the budget. In fact, we began to break even. It was a remarkably successful salvage, if I say so myself.

Q: Charlotte, were you involved in the great New Canaan fluoride crisis of 1958. Fluoride goes into most toothpaste nowadays, but at one time it was very controversial.

CB: Oh, that was quite an episode! The League of Women Voters invited me to tell them about sewage, and on the same program Mr. A. Leland Glidden gave a talk about water. He was president of the New Canaan Water Company, and everyone called him Buddy. One of the women asked him, "Have you ever thought about putting fluoride in the water?" He looked at me, and then answered, "Yes, we're going to put

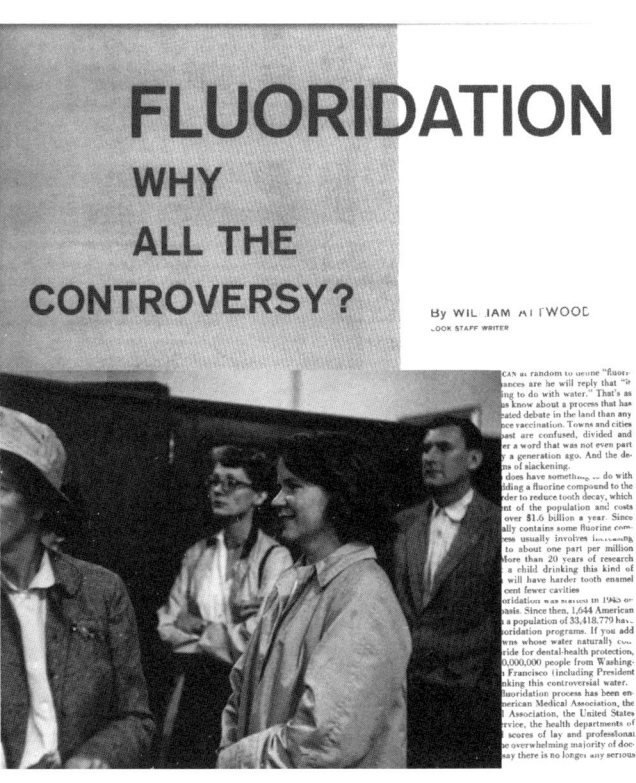

1958: Dr. Charlotte Brown (raincoat) at the fluoridation debate

fluoride in the water." Both of us thought Buddy would just call Hartford and find out how to do it, and then do it. But there were women in the League who were going to see that it didn't happen. Buddy Glidden, for his part, had a kind of spiritual feeling about it, I think. At one point when the opposition was building up I said to him, "How can you stand all this fighting?" and Buddy said, "This is the only opportunity I have ever had in my life to do something for somebody, and we are going to do it!" That's how he felt.

David and I went to see the new professor of public health at Cornell, Walsh McDermott, and told him how we were running into resistance. He said, "If you can't do it in New Canaan, they can't do it here in New York City. And in New York it's very important." He picked up the phone and called the person in charge of water supply at the U.S. Public Health Service in Washington. This man flew right up to see us in New Canaan.

Q: What was the opposition like?

CB: A woman named Martha Barnes knew that fluoridation was bad, and she had money to finance a campaign to stop it. She organized a coalition of organic gardeners, Christian Scientists, and other people who were just against new things generally. The DAR and other patriots got involved; to some of them it smelled like a Communist plot! We formed our own committee. Kay Lusk, who was big in the League of Women Voters, and Carl Black, just retired as head of American Can Company, were co-chairs. A man whose day job was public relations joined the committee. I heard that the opposition had found a man in Seattle, Dr. Frederick Exter, to fly to New Canaan and debate with me about the pros and cons of putting fluoride in the water. Mrs. Barnes was going to pay his fare. So I called an emergency meeting of our committee, and Hank — our PR man — said that agreeing to a public debate against a skilled propagandist was not a good idea; this guy had done this many times before, and he knew all the tricks. Hank said, "I want you to write a letter to every professor of preventive dentistry in the country, every professor of public health in the major medical schools, every commissioner of health of a big city. Ask them all to come and debate this man. Then get your friend at the Public Health Service to write these same people, saying, 'You are going to get a letter from a Dr.

Brown, the health director of a small town, which you might ordinarily throw away, but I want you to answer it. Even if you don't agree to come, tell her what you would say if you could come." It was a brilliant idea. The letters we got back were wonderful!

Q: What happened then?

CB: The opposition organized a petition for a town referendum. A debate was set up at Saxe Junior High School on May 2, 1958, the night before the referendum. There was a big crowd. By this time *Look* magazine was interested. (William Attwood was in on this; he was their national editor at the time.) They sent out a team to cover the meeting and referendum, and afterwards they ran a lead article by Bill Attwood, with a lot of pictures. The Seattle man did his stuff, and when it came my turn to speak, Carl Black — that heavenly man! — stood up with great dignity and this whole sheaf of letters. And he said, "I will just choose a few of these to read to you." He read some of the best ones, and that ended the debate.

Buddy Glidden's mind was already made up. "Our board of directors has voted for fluoridation," he told me after the debate. "I don't give a damn how people vote tomorrow. I'm going to go ahead with it anyhow. If they don't feel like drinking our water, they can drink something else." If he had said this at the meeting, it might have caused a little trouble, but of course he didn't.

We won the referendum, by more than two to one as I recall, and New Canaan got fluoridated water. And the eyes of the country were on public health in our community — at least for that week.

~~~~~

On March 30, 2001, Dr. David Brown addressed the Poinsettia Club quarterly dinner on the topic: "Perspectives on New Canaan's Characteristics from a Half-Century of Medical Practice." Here is part of what he said:

"When you think about it, medical practice is an excellent way for people to discover each other and to expose a physician to the qualities of a town and his neighbors. One by one, people come to a doctor believing (hoping) he may help them feel better. The doctor meets them with some training and insights which he bravely hopes will be useful. Both of them, through trust and faith, reject their obvious inadequacies and face the risk of failure, to create a very intimate relationship. Personal facades — status, political, religious, race, etc. — fade in this ambiance of mutual hope. Much of what is special about a person and a community come into view.

"Counting it all up, seeing twenty patients a day gave me at least 180,000 intimate contacts with New Canaanites over my years of active practice. But what I did and learned in those years was small compared to what New Canaan's people risked, tried and established. A town's government does not necessarily respond with enthusiasm to proposals for health care innovations and service facilities emanating from the private sector. Meals on Wheels, the VNA, Waveny Care Center, New Canaan Inn, Schoolhouse Apartments, the Ambulance Corps, the Lapham Community Center — to name some — were largely initiated and supported by the energy, faith, dedication and vision of our town's remarkable people. . .

"Practice remains a moving experience for me. It was always instructive, gratifying and humbling, but it was also beset with surprisingly unexpected and undeserved moments of joy, sorrow, humor, pathos, frustration and grief. I never knew enough — no doctor ever does — never fully understood why some of my guesses worked so well (or so poorly). Along the way I came to realize that my profession chooses and molds its practitioners — not the other way around. I finished practice reluctantly and remain awed, humbled and honored to have had the privilege of helping wonderful people do wonderful things."

(Traditionally, members of the august Poinsettia Club are not given to effusive demonstrations of approval or affection. On this valedictory occasion, we are told, they rose for a standing ovation.)

The Browns on a medical mission to the West Bank and Gaza in 1995. Here they are sightseeing near the Dead Sea.

5 Nine to Five and Beyond: The Business Scene

Joseph C. Sweet

Newcomers to New Canaan half a century ago were struck by the number of liquor stores — fifteen. Today we are down to four, two of them adjuncts to supermarkets. Newcomers these days remark on the plethora of real estate firms and antique shops, not to mention the availability of good coffee from the likes of Starbuck's, Zumbach's and Dunkin' Donuts. Our businesses in 1950, largely retail merchants and services, were mainly clustered around Main and Elm Streets — the "Village." When you walked down the street, you knew most of the people you met, and you greeted them. In the shops and banks you were addressed cordially by name. Several food stores, including Totaro's, Gristede's and Rosen's, took orders by telephone, made home deliveries, and billed their regular customers monthly. Time marches on.

Apart from grocery chains like the A&P and First National, local people owned and managed most of the stores, gas stations and other service providers. Downtown parking usually presented no great problem. Most everyday shopping could be done locally. The G. C. Murphy outlet on Elm Street opposite South Avenue was a typical "5&10" offering a multitude of household needs. It was supplanted in 1957 by Thornton Fuller's, a select department store, which succumbed in 1974 to competition from out-of-town discounters like Caldor's. Gillane's, a dry goods store on Main Street, folded in 1980. Walter Stewart's Market, founded in 1907 and still in the Stewart family, is a hearty survivor, but there aren't many like it.

A Parcel of Old-Timers

Several of our inns have venerable roots. The Holmewood Inn, which opened in 1925 on Oenoke Ridge, was bought in 1960 by a direct descendant of Roger Sherman, the Connecticut Revolutionary statesman, and named after him. The building itself dates back to the mid-1700s. The Maples Inn, which began life in

1908 as the Hampton Inn, was renamed by a new owner in 1982. The Village Inn, also dating from 1908, was owned and operated as the Melba Inn by three generations of the Bach family until it was sold and given its new name in 1998.

The New Canaan Water Company was incorporated in 1893 by local residents to dam the Five Mile River, forming a reservoir between Smith and Oenoke Ridges. Its long-time principal owner and president, A. Leland ("Buddy") Glidden, fought successfully to add fluoride to the town's water system in the 1950s. (See "Health of a Community," p. 43). The Company is now a subsidiary of the Kelda Group PLC, a multinational British water-supply concern. Scofield's Furniture Store, at Main Street and Burtis Avenue, was established in 1900 and is still in the Scofield family. The Town's oldest real estate firm is Brotherhood & Higley, founded by John Brotherhood in 1926.

The New Canaan Drug Store, one of the oldest in the state, was opened in 1845 on the west side of Main Street opposite East Avenue. The original structure was demolished in 1965 when Main Street was widened. The store's interior, all but the soda fountain, was salvaged and removed to the Historical Society, where it survives in effigy as a museum exhibit in a wing of its own. The pharmacy, now Varnum's, continues at the same location; in 1997 it became a setting for a major motion picture. (See "Ice Storm in A Teacup," p. 93).

Jake Bertram opened the Modern Barber Shop (actually an *old-fashioned* barber shop) in 1938. He and his son Albert moved it around the corner from Main Street to Burtis Avenue in 1965. Albert's son Bruce later joined the family business — another three-generation New Canaan business enterprise. Sold in 1995, it has been replaced by Lisa's Classic Cuts. Franco's Wine Merchants on Elm Street, which dates back to 1936, is still owned and managed by members of the Franco family, expanding its market reach far beyond the town. Its newer neighbor, the prestigious Whitney Shop, has been on Elm Street since 1946. As Judy Stinchfield's upscale women's clothing and gift business prospered, it spread into its present elegant premises.

Nine to Five and Beyond: The Business Scene

Don Hersam, Jr., perched on the roof of his office, flanked by John Hersam (left) and Marty Hersam. In the doorway below are Jeanne Hersam (left) and Mary Anne Hersam.

The *New Canaan Advertiser* was founded in 1908 by John E. Hersam. The current publisher is Hersam's grandson, V. Donald Hersam, Jr., and the latter's son Martin joined the business in 1988 — a four generation spread. After many years on Elm Street, the newspaper moved in 1972 to a new building on Vitti Street. The paper's old premises were first leased to Fat Tuesday, a trendy restaurant, then to a bank, and recently to another restaurant, Solé. (For restaurants, see "Town Restaurants Revisited," p. 67). The neighboring New Canaan Playhouse has been a fixture in the town's recreational scene since it opened in 1923. In 1986 the building was refurbished and "twinned," so that two movies can be shown simultaneously. In 2000 the owner, Hoyt Cinema Corp., announced plans to sell the property with a restriction that it could never again be used as a movie house. After much public stir and negotiation, it was sold to the Franco Family Trust and Jeroll Silverberg, and Hoyt Cinema has agreed to lease and operate it as a movie theater for seven more years.

The New Canaan Book Shop was started in 1959 in an empty storefront in the oldest then-existing building on Elm Street. Once a livery stable, later a funeral parlor, it was replaced in 1978 by the present brick structure, where the business survives in the top ranks of quality local book stores of the region, if not of the country.

The Hoyt Funeral Home has been in its present quarters on south Main Street since 1930. Having changed hands many times, it retains the name of one of its earlier proprietors, Franklin B. Hoyt. The Silvermine Market, a variety store and delicatessen just across from the entrance to the Silvermine Guild Arts Center, has been around since 1887, when this horse-and-buggy town consisted of eleven separate hamlets with their own schools, shops and other services. The business was "grandfathered" when residential zoning restrictions were introduced early in the last century. It has recently been sold and the new owner will continue its operation while adding a catering service.

CARS FOR SALE

There are only two automobile franchises here these days, Griffin Ford and Karl Chevrolet, down from three since the disappearance of Karl Buick in 1971. The Ford agency, established here about 1938, acquired its present name when it changed owners in 1960. The Chevrolet agency, started in 1927 by Leo and Emil Karl toward the western end of Elm Street, has expanded continually over the years. Leo Karl, Jr., took over after his father's death in 1952, and Leo Karl, III, became the official "dealer" in 1996. Recently the firm was franchised to sell the huge Hummer utility vehicles. In 1971 another member of the family, Richard Karl, and a partner opened a Saab agency on Vitti Street. It closed in 1981. The Karl family and its enterprises have long been recognized as leading sponsors of New Canaan civic and community causes.

In the early 1960s Elm Street west of the railroad station briefly began to take on the appearance of "automobile row" as two new dealerships opened: Colonial Motors of New Canaan, a Mercedes franchise which lasted only until 1965, and New Canaan Imported Cars, which offered a variety of British makes from 1960 to 1963. On the other side of town, Thompson Motors sold Pontiacs and G.M.C. trucks for four years in the 1950s at the corner of Locust Avenue and Forest Street.

Lindner Cycle Shop, founded in Stamford in 1949 by Gordon Lindner, has maintained a quiet but impressive presence on Forest Street since 1961. It is one of the oldest BMW dealerships—if not the oldest—in the nation. The storefront features the original shop sign.

BANKS: A TANGLED WEB

In 1950 New Canaan had only two banks, the New Canaan Savings Bank, founded in 1859, and the First National Bank of New Canaan, which opened in 1865. The past half-century has seen many changes not only in these two old-timers, but also a proliferation of other banks, and a maze of mergers and acquisitions that provide a challenge for even the most diligent researcher. What can be offered here is only an outline.

The story of the New Canaan Savings Bank is comparatively straightforward. It merged into the Mechanics and Farmers Bank of Bridgeport in 1982, which nine years later was taken over by Chase Manhattan Bank of Connecticut. The evolution of the First National Bank of New Canaan, on the other hand, is more tortuous. By the 1950s its name had become the First National Bank and Trust Company of New Canaan. Soon thereafter it merged into the Fairfield County Trust Company, which was in turn taken over in 1968 by Union Trust, a subsidiary of New England Bankcorp, Inc. Since the 1990s even further consolidation has taken place, but we must cut to the chase: the sign on the handsome brick building across Main Street from the Library, which until recently read "Union Trust," now says "First Union." However, a further change in name and ownership is presently in the news.

Meanwhile other banks saw an opportunity in this affluent community. The first of these, in 1958, was the National Bank & Trust Company of Fairfield County. In 1962 its name was changed to State National Bank of Connecticut. Ten years later it merged with and became a branch of the Connecticut Bank and Trust Company. That bank in turn was taken over in 1991 by Fleet Bank, which merged with the Bank of Boston in 2000 to become Fleet Boston Financial Corp., but continues under the name Fleet. In 1965 the Connecticut National Bank opened its 39th branch here, and in 1989 it added another local one. In 1992 the bank was absorbed by Shawmut National Corp., and both branches went by that name until Shawmut was taken over by Fleet in 1996.

In the mid-1970s a group of local residents started the New Canaan Bank and Trust Company at 208 Elm Street. It prospered, and in 1990 a branch was opened at the corner of Locust Avenue and Forest Street. The Summit Bank (of New Jersey) bought both offices in 1999, and Summit in turn was acquired by Fleet in early 2001. In 1980 Guardian Savings and Loan opened a branch here; four years later Guardian was absorbed by People's Bank (of Bridgeport), whose New Canaan branch now occupies the site on Main Street where the Gran Central Market used to be. In 1988 the Stamford Savings Bank opened an office here, and promptly changed its name to First County Bank, which recently took over the small bank building on Park Street adjacent to the station. The most recent newcomer is Putnam Trust, a division of the Bank of New York; in 1999 it moved into the storefront space at 86 Elm Street previously occupied by First County.

In 2000 a group of residents decided to start a new bank here, the Bank of New Canaan. It is expected to open later this year at the northeast corner of East Avenue and Cherry Street.

HARDWARE, BUILDING SUPPLIES AND A TREE NURSERY

Silliman's Hardware, which in 1950 occupied the wedge-shaped, four-story corner building at Main Street and Forest, began in 1867 as a grocery but over the years segued into a first-class hardware store. In time, however, competition from discount chains and shopping centers took their toll, and Silliman's closed in 1981. Weed & Duryea, which began as a planing mill and lumberyard in 1868 but later developed a small hardware sales operation, was a beneficiary; its hardware sales tripled after Silliman's closed, and the expanding business moved to its present Grove Street building. Another competitor, New Canaan Fuel and Lumber, headed from 1937 by Earl M. Smith, Sr., eventually controlled three real estate firms, three gas stations, and various other commercial properties, including the New Canaan Racquet Club. In 1968 Earl Smith, Jr., took over from his father as president and added a home-owner's building supplies retail center. Both it and the lumberyard closed down in 1990, and the latter was moved to Newtown. In the mid 1960s plans had been announced to build an office complex on the local lumberyard site, to be called "New Canaan Plaza." After a long zoning struggle, building permits were obtained but the office buildings were never erected. In 1995 Avalon Communities bought the property, proposing to create a large apartment complex there. After much controversy, lengthy negotiations, and a hotly contested referendum, the Town and Avalon made a swap. The Avalon housing development will rise on former Town land off Lakeview Avenue overlooking Mill Pond, while the former lumberyard property will soon become a commuter parking lot.

Hoyt's Nursery, with origins in the early nineteenth century and under one-family ownership for 125 years, was at one time the largest tree nursery in New England. At its peak it covered about 600 acres in the southeastern quarter of the town (almost twice the size of the Waveny estate) and employed more than fifty men, who were housed on the property dormitory-style, with kitchen and dining facilities. In the 1960s it was decided to sell the property, by then reduced to a little over 250 acres. The state's Development Commission proposed a local "limited" airport on the site, but nothing came of the idea. An affiliate of Sears Roebuck obtained an option to buy the land to construct a large shopping mall, but that plan also fell through. Both Xerox and RCA had their eyes on the nursery land for a corporate

Nine to Five and Beyond: The Business Scene

headquarters, and in 1971 RCA bought it for about three million dollars. Predictably, as the entire area was in the two-acre residential zone, a zoning battle ensued. In the end, RCA resold the property to the D'Addario firm of Bridgeport, which turned the old nursery property into the residential development known as Hoyt Farms.

A Tale of Two Dairies

In 1950 New Canaan had two dairies, neither of which was to survive the century. The Norman Dairy was on Weed Street at the corner of Old Stamford road, and Miller's was on lower Ponus Ridge. Dating from 1914, Norman's became one of the area's largest, with eight milk routes. In January 1946 both of them were involved in the most bitter labor dispute in town history, when sixty-five cars carrying 200 members of the International Brotherhood of Teamsters, AFL, appeared from out of town to picket them. The Teamsters' effort to unionize the dairies was supported by a local group called the People's Union.

The dispute was eventually settled, but increased labor costs, competition from large dairies, and reduced demand for home milk deliveries led to their eventual demise. The Miller Dairy closed in 1971, and Norman's in 1974. For some years the Norman facilities and buildings remained idle, and were repeatedly vandalized. In 1982 the deteriorating structures, having been declared unsafe by Town officials, were all demolished except for one barn, which remains on the site as the nucleus of the Elise Nursery, opened in 1983.

Closed for the holiday: the farm stand at Fairty orchard

Another vanished remnant of New Canaan's agricultural past was the Fairty farm and apple orchard on Old Stamford Road just south of the Village. Apples and other produce were on sale at a roadside stand, but in the autumn it was a special treat to drive into the farmyard and watch the fragrant old wooden cider press at work. The operation closed in 1987, to be replaced by a residential development.

From Dickerman's to Breslow's to MacKenzie's

Two other businesses that did not survive the century were Dickerman's and Breslow's. Dickerman's opened on Main Street in 1891 as a news and stationery store. Having changed hands many times over the years, by the time it closed in 1991 it was known as

~61~

the only place in town to get a typewriter cleaned and repaired — by then a service going the way of the buggy-whip. Breslow's was something else: in business on Elm Street since 1938, it became the closest thing the Village had to a universal variety store. It sometimes seemed that Mr. Breslow carried everything. ("Need some ping-pong balls on Sunday morning? Try Breslow's.") It was understood that if Mr. Breslow spotted a child he knew lifting a candy bar without paying for it, he would simply add it to the parents' monthly bill. In 1978 the Breslow family sold out; the stationery store continued another two decades as Jackson's, but it was never quite the same. The space on Elm Street is now occupied by the distinctly upmarket La Plume Doree, which carries "luxury stationery, quality pens and fine library appointments," but not ping-pong balls.

Another shop that developed its own niche was the Corner Cigar Store on Elm Street (where Baskin-Robbins is now), which carried a large stock of pre-Castro Havana cigars. Affecting the role of a curmudgeon, owner Sam Silverberg had a sign in the window that said "Where the Customer Is Always Wrong!" Sam closed the store in 1967 after fifty years in business.

The de facto successor of Breslow's is MacKenzie's, opened by Malcolm MacKenzie in 1977 on South Avenue. Its original name has survived several owners. It is notable for a wide selection of magazines and out-of-town newspapers, office supplies and stationery, and a copying machine that generally works — also steaming coffee before dawn for a daily cluster of congenial insomniacs, just about the only thing Breslow's never thought of.

CLUB 31 AND IZZY'S PLACE

From 1945 to 1969 Ed Janis ran an unremarkable men's haberdashery at 31 Elm Street whose chief claim to fame was a back room with a potbellied stove that was never fired up. Ed's back room was called "Club 31" or the "Town Hall Annex" on account of the gatherings and discussions that took place

---

How Can Pierre's Prices Be So Low?

Considering the superb cuisine, the choice wines from far flung vineyards, and the Continental atmosphere of the Zebra Room, the world traveler may well ask, "How can Pierre's prices be so low?"

The answer exposes a well-kept family secret.

Izzy Piere Cohen, the arbiter of New Canaan's smart set, totes up the checks at Pierre's—and Izzy can't count above ten without taking his shoes off!

Pierre's

Izzy's Place

NEW   CANAAN

(Placed by Pierre's "Skeleton in Closet" Dept.)

Nine to Five and Beyond: The Business Scene

around that cold stove. Local politicians, attorneys, bankers, real estate brokers and other wheelers and dealers would congregate there in mid-morning for coffee and — it was said — to settle policy matters that were not yet quite ripe for ventilating at Town Hall or in the press.

At 39 Elm Street, near Club 31, was Pierre's, truly a landmark watering hole. It had its origins after the Prohibition era as Doyle's Tavern, owned by Joe Doyle, who was blind. In 1937 Doyle hired Israel ("Izzy") Cohen as manager. Within a year Cohen turned the business around so that it was actually making money, and when Doyle died in 1944, his heirs gave Izzy the business in recognition of his loyalty and integrity. "Izzy's Place" attracted both a blue-collar and a white-collar clientele, who gathered there to discuss community topics. Its nucleus was a "round table" for luncheon regulars, and it provided other refreshment for weary commuters as they emerged from the home-bound train out of Madison Avenue and environs. (For more on the cuisine and atmosphere see "Town Restaurants Revisited," p. 67).

Izzy had bought the tavern building and in 1953, when the next door Chinese laundry closed, he expanded his operation there with a full-scale restaurant. Local artist and decorator E. Kenyon Davies volunteered to design the interior, incorporating a black-and-white zebra-striped wall treatment inspired by the fabled El Morocco night club in New York (see "Visual Artists," p. 127). A new name, Pierre's, was adopted, proposed by a patron who had been reading *Holiday* magazine. But Izzy was not all business. He sponsored local youth programs and sports teams, invariably known as the New Canaan Zebras. (See "Youth Must Be Served," p. 97). During World War II he sent a regular newsletter to young New Canaan men and women in the armed services throughout the world, and shipped them regular supplies of cigarettes and candy. When the war was over, he hosted what was said to be the

Two of a long series of newspaper ads for Izzy's Place created by regular customers from the advertising world

---

"If You're Looking For That Je Ne Sais Quoi. I Got A Bucketful Of It"

Says Izzy, Maitre d'Cafe de Pierre.

"Maybe I got two bucketsful," continues this popular raconteur, wit, and arbtier of the New Canaan smart set.

"Why be what you are all your life? Enjoy the continental atmosphere, the unexcelled cuisine and the "je ne sais quoi" in a cocktail glass at Pierre's.

Also—Why have macaroni at home again?

Pierre's
(Izzy's Place)

ELM STREET   NEW CANAAN

New Canaan 9-9056

biggest outdoor party in the history of the town — a clam bake with roast beef and all the "fixins" on Moller's Field.

Izzy Cohen sold his place in 1962, and the following year he was honored by his friends, customers and peers as the local Gridiron Club's third fall guy

~~~~~~~~

Owing to space limitations, Joseph C. Sweet's review of business in New Canaan, 1950-2000, unfortunately had to be condensed for this publication. His original manuscript, with further information on all the businesses mentioned here, plus many others, is on file at the library of the Historical Society. Mr. Sweet, a retired IBM lawyer, is the town historian and a prolific Historical Society author. He recently retired as the longtime leader of the town band.

Elm Street shops about 1970

6   Rosen's: A Slice of Old New Canaan

Jane Caulfield

For over half a century Rosen Brothers Market was a thriving business at 80 Main Street in New Canaan. Fifty-six years after its opening, in the fall of 1986, its doors were closed. It is said customers wept and kissed the grocer good-bye. This was the end of an era that was to be replaced by acres of supermarket space and computerized check-out in our thriving town.

Rosen's market was a store with three small aisles, wood floors and one lone register. The shelves were stocked, however, with as many groceries as most full-size supermarkets of the day would hold. You could get at least six kinds of peanut butter and most brands of beer. Every flavor of gelatin was available, and there were dozens of specialty items for favorite customers. While not the oldest food store in town (Stewart's was about twice its age and still in the same family), Rosen's was the first to carry meats and abundant supplies of produce and canned goods. If something was not in stock, it would be ordered one day and received and delivered the next, or a speedy clerk would fetch an order from the friendly GranCentral across the street and deliver it to a customer.

But what was most special about Rosen's was its devoted "club" of customers. It was a gathering place for many clients and their children. Clerks, considered friends, knew the customers by names and appetites. Pleasantries were exchanged across the meat counter, clerks would watch children while their parents shopped, and despite the availability of grocery carts, most customers sought the assistance of a clerk to walk and shop through the store with them. ("Women didn't like the carts, however," the Rosens recalled.) It was not unusual to place one's order by phone for pick-up and delivery, and something as simple as a pound of sugar or as grand as a month's provisions might be asked to be delivered. They were even known to put a delivered order in the refrigerator. And at this time Rosen's was the only place in town where one could have a charge account. In this old-fashioned grocery store was a quality often compared to a small Vermont country store where shopping was unhurried, a pleasure and an outing.

At the heart of Rosen's Market was the Rosen family with two generations managing the store. The last owners were Harvey Lapin and Joan Rosen Lapin. It was Helen Rosen, wife of the store's founder, Leo Rosen, who said at its closing, "Now we're the last of our kind." Several New Canaan families had been customers for four generations and many for three. Family joys and sorrows were mutually shared. There are those who remember leaving their shopping lists to be filled by a clerk or a family member while they did other errands in the Village. Rosen's closed because the owners were looking for a less exhausting life, and they felt the only way a business like this could work was if it were a family business. They felt their options were limited. Rosen's devoted customers wondered if anything would ever be the same

Modern supermarkets noted for their bounty and glitter, for their efficiency and computerized speed serve our multitude of needs in this present-day, fast-paced world. But how many of us weep when any one supermarket closes? Rosen Brothers Market was truly a village institution, a real super market.

(This article has drawn on Kathy Wagner's coverage of Rosen's closing in the Advertiser, *Sept. 25, 1986)*

Jane Caulfield has lived in New Canaan for over 30 years, raising children, teaching and volunteering in the community.

Rosen's market just before it closed in 1986. From the left: Helen Rosen, Joan Rosen Lapin and Harvey Lapin.

7 Town Restaurants Revisited

Patricia Brooks

Photos of Patricia Brooks are rare, because she visits restaurants incognito. The hat here is one of her disguises.

If a former resident were to return to New Canaan today, after a fifty-year absence, one of the first things to surprise and amaze might be the transformation of the town's restaurant scene. For one thing, there now is a scene, whereas in the 1950s to as late as the 1970s there were few dining options in town. Fine dining, as contrasted with mere eating, that is. Out-of-towners in New Canaan for a day of shopping and antiquing were hard pressed to find a restaurant downtown that was casual and yet presentable. Many settled for a sandwich from the Deli-Bake.

Restaurant food of that era was, by today's standards, mundane. The most exciting menu-offering in town was sauerbraten, to be found at the Roger Sherman Inn, the town's only star in the gustatory firmament. Sauerbraten and veal cordon bleu. Contrast that with what's available at New Canaan restaurants in the year 2001: lemon grass chicken, sushi and sashimi, tandoori lamb, grilled octopus, calamari fritti, farfalle con funghi, buffalo burgers, empanadas, yucca fritters and tortilla soup, seafood risotto, jambalaya, gumbo, to cite just a few dishes. The list goes on, the fresh and foreign ingredients endless. We live in a different century, a different world.

This is now, that was then. Back then, and for many years, the Roger Sherman Inn was under the stewardship of Steven Zur and was a quiet oasis of continental cuisine. When Zur and his partner, Mrs. Catherine Maliszewski, sold the inn in 1988 to Henry H. Prieger, French cuisine, as featured at Prieger's Inn at Ridgefield, became the hallmark. Since 1997, this old New Canaan landmark has sparkled under the ownership of Thomas and Kay Weilenmann, with Swiss/French the dominant cuisine de la maison.

In the old days — the deprived old days culinarily speaking — the Roger Sherman was it for elegant dining. But for local color, no place equaled Pierre's on Elm Street. Known to everyone as Izzy's Place, after owner Israel Cohen, this was a favorite hangout of locals and commuters alike. Postmen after making their deliveries, policemen, local workers and commuters just off the train stopped in for a late afternoon round or two at Izzy's long bar. Local politicos had their own reserved table for lunch in the front window of the bar and woe be to anyone who tried to sit down there by mistake. On any given weekday, Judge Julius Groher, Selectman Pete Raymond and others could be seen gabbing and gossiping over their sandwiches. The ladies who lunch ate in Izzy's more sedate dining room, but the bar was the place for the regulars. Palate appeal was secondary, but at least one old-timer still recalls with a sense of loss Izzy's bacon-lettuce-and-tomato sandwiches. Donald Hersam, publisher of the *New Canaan Advertiser*, recalls the evening when he ran into Douglas Edwards, CBS newscaster and New Canaan resident, there and they swapped stories and opinions until the bar closed. When Izzy's shut its doors for the last time in 1976 the loss was mourned all over New Canaan (if not by resident gourmets). Some diehards vowed never to cross the threshold of Family Britches, the clothing store that replaced it.

A corner table at Izzy's

Meanwhile, little by little a few other restaurants opened. Making the biggest — perhaps the only — splash in the early 1970s was Fat Tuesday, whose day-before-Ash Wednesday name had to be explained to many local residents. In 1973 it took over the *New Canaan Advertiser's* old office and plant at 105 Elm Street, and the cavernous space became open and airy in the faux-New Orleans Mardi Gras mode. Actor Robert Mitchum, long rumored to be a partner, was there for opening night. Fat Tuesday lasted until 1988, but by then the restaurant scene was achanging. Today, its spacious interior, now the bailiwick of Solé Ristorante, has been re-created as an Italian villa.

Some of Izzy's faithful discovered and settled in at Cherry Street East, the successor to the Town restaurant at 45 East Avenue, which opened around 1978 and remains a popular hang-out bar where simple meals are also served.

A milestone date in the restaurant annals of New Canaan was 1979 when William (Billy) Auer and two partners launched Gates at 10 Forest Street, which quickly became the upscale Izzy's of the upcoming decades. Sightings there of Robert Redford, Sylvester Stallone and other non-New Canaan celebrities added to the allure

Town Restaurants Revisited

of this new, casual and lively place. New Canaan young people loved (still do) the bar and the beer selection and others liked the clubby tables where they could watch most of New Canaan dining at one time or another.

The 1980s saw a number of restaurant openings. In 1982 Mr. Lee, established by local condominium builder Johnson Lee, was New Canaan's first upscale Chinese restaurant, established in the transformed premises of the old Martin's clothing store on Main Street. This was New Canaan's first classy Chinese restaurant and it was decidedly elegant. A much publicized episode, in which many Mr. Lee staffers, recently arrived Chinese emigrants, were rounded up in a raid by the INS, may have led to the restaurant's demise.

The restaurant and food revolution overtaking the United States in the late 1980s inched its way to New Canaan as well. An attractive, much remodeled house at 183 Cherry Street, where the Heritage, a homey mom-and-pop style Italian restaurant, once held sway, opened as Bogey's, then in 1986 morphed into Mulligan's, and in 1998 became Logan's. It is no more.

The restaurant business, never known for stability, brought its share of openings, closings and revolving doors to downtown New Canaan. An obvious example is the former Veterans' Hall, the imposing colonnaded building at 62 Main Street opposite Town Hall. In 1988 the premises were occupied by Lissard House, an antiques emporium-cum-tearoom. A year later, L'Abbee moved into the space and remained there until the late 1990s. Then White Oak Bistro opened in 1999 and survived less than a year, to be followed in 2000 by 62 Main Street, the current occupant.

Nantucket Cafe opened in 1987 in minuscule premises at 15 Elm Street, formerly occupied by Libby's Diner, and moved in 1990 to much larger quarters at 6 Forest Street, next door to Gates. Nantucket Cafe gave way in 1993 to Tequila Mocking Bird, another of Billy Auer's enterprises. Tequila Mocking Bird turned the former New England-themed interior into a colorful Mexican market scene, which it remains today. Meanwhile, Blue Water Cafe has been happily entrenched in Nantucket Cafe's original tiny quarters on Elm Street since 1990. Among its devoted regulars is architect Philip Johnson.

If one were to believe the theory that some locations are spooked, another building that saw various restaurant turnovers was the New Canaan Racquet Club at 45 Grove Street, alongside the railroad tracks. Beginning as Huckleberry's, which opened in spacious rooms there in 1978, the premises saw a number of tenants, from Sneakers to Stone Horse to Mac's Grill Room, the last resident, which disbanded in 1999.

It was really the 1990s when the U.S. culinary revolution exploded with gusto in New Canaan. Prezzo came along in 1991 and, with its Italian menu and pizzas, settled into the lower level of the building at 2 Forest Street that once housed Silliman's department store. In 1999 Billy Auer and partners unveiled the cozy French-style Bistro Bonne Nuit at 12 Forest Street. Rigoletto at 26 Locust Avenue gave way to Mattie's family restaurant.

Meanwhile around the corner on Main Street, the 1990s were a real happening. The Bank on Main Street, at 87 Main, in the premises long occupied by Union Trust, opened in 1997, but had a short life, succeeded in 2000 by Tandoori Taste of India, New Canaan's first Indian restaurant. Across the street the Little Kitchen of New Canaan, in Mr. Lee's old spot, opened in 1989, followed in quick succession by three other Chinese/South Asian establishments, Asie in 1998 and in 1999 Sentosa, then Ching's Table, which seems to have taken up residence permanently.

Another opening, another show. In a single decade, New Canaan turned from a minimal restaurant town into one of Fairfield County's major dining-out magnets. Here in brief is why: two Chinese restaurants (Hunan Taste and Magic Wok, both on Elm Street), one Japanese (Plum Tree at 70 Main), one Chinese/Malaysian/Thai (Ching's Table), one Indian (Thali), two French (Roger Sherman Inn and Bistro Bonne Nuit), Italian (Prezzo, Vicolo on Main Street, and Solé), Modern American (62 Main Street, Gates, Blue Water Cafe), one Mexican (Tequila Mocking Bird). In addition, there are assorted sandwich shops, pizzerias, delis, muffin, donut, bakery and coffee shops, gourmet take-outs and even short order places, totaling close to thirty food purveyors. It is difficult even to remember the days when New Canaan was considered, in one restaurateur's view, a bland "white bread town" where no ethnic restaurants dare tread.

Town Restaurants Revisited

A restaurant town, New Canaan? In 1950 it was beyond any resident's wildest dreams. Older residents will remember how the downtown streets were usually deserted most evenings after the shops and offices had closed. But a walk along Elm and Main Streets between 6 and 8 p.m. nowadays is like being in a mini-SoHo, with groups of people — families, couples, quartets — all meandering to a restaurant of choice. It's a long way, both gourmetwise and in real time, from the era of Paggy's and Libby's Diner to the New Canaan of the year 2001.

Patricia Brooks and her husband Lester have lived here since 1959. Her reviews of Connecticut restaurants have appeared in the New York Times every Sunday since 1977.

Texture of a Community

"Sledding on Benedict Hill" by Walter DuBois Richards

8 The Schools of a Community

with Betty Quinn and Hudson Stoddard

Leaving aside the picturesque but anachronistic one-room Little Red Schoolhouse on Carter Street (closed in 1957), in the school year 1949-50 all three of New Canaan's public school buildings were an easy walk from "the Village." Those three have since been converted into affordable housing, a police headquarters, and a parking lot. Our five present-day school buildings were built during the last half-century, all at a good distance from the town center. Since 1950 New Canaan's population has grown from 8,001 to 19,395, while public school enrollment has increased from 1,450 to 3,549.

Statistics like these surely reflect change and expansion. But behind the buildings and the numbers is a constant theme — the evolution of public education in a town that never lost sight of the value of excellence, benefiting always from constructive collaboration among dedicated professionals, elected officials, and informed citizens. That symbiosis helps explain why our town's school system is consistently rated among the best in the state and in the nation; why real estate agents use these ratings to lure young families to the town; why taxpayers with little direct interest in what goes on in the schoolroom — well, most of them anyhow — do not begrudge the costs.

The most direct link between the schools and the Town is the Board of Education, instituted in 1894 after New Canaan voted to consolidate its existing eleven district schools under one administration. Other than the Town Council, the elected Board of Ed is arguably the most representative public body we have. Connecticut state law designates the superintendent of schools as the "chief executive officer" of the school system. This is a three-year appointment by the board carrying with it management of the lion's share of the Town budget and also its highest salary, but the board is required by law to "evaluate" the superintendent every year, so the relationship is bound to be close. It is extraordinary that over the past fifty years New Canaan has changed superintendents only three times. How many public school systems have enjoyed that kind of continuity of leadership?

To achieve perspective on fifty years of educational achievement the Society has drawn on two veterans. Betty Quinn, now retired, was for many years a middle-school science teacher and administrator in New Canaan. She combines hands-on knowledge of what was happening "within the system" with the insights of a professional educator into the role of public education in society. Hudson Stoddard has been involved with our public schools almost since he and his family moved here in 1956. Elected to the Board of Education in 1959, he served for eight years, including two terms as chairman. In the 1990s he renewed his involvement as a member of the Town Council.

~~~~~

Each of our present schoolhouses has its own story. South School, designed by New Canaan architect Willis Mills and opened in late 1950, was the first that was "modern" in style, with its flat roof, open classrooms, and curtain walls of glass. It was widely emulated during the post-War II school-building boom. (One teacher there recalls school officials from as far away as California pressing their faces against the windows of her classroom to see what was going on inside!) West School and then East School followed soon after. Center School, showing its age since its construction in 1909, was declared

Center School, demolished in 1983. The site is now a parking lot occupied by a farmers' market each summer Saturday.

8:10 a.m. at West School. Katie Campbell draws while Rebecca Britton practices violin and David Campbell checks music. A Syd Greenberg classic from the Advertiser.

redundant and demolished in 1983, much to the dismay of sentimental former students and their parents. But population projections being as unreliable as they are, as Hudson Stoddard observes, it was not long before all three remaining primary schools required additions. And recently, as in the past, it is hard for some parents to accept the concept that the school your children attend depends on which street they call home.

High school classes over the years have been led a rather merry chase. Before 1927, students had to trek to Stamford — a train ride followed by a considerable hike. In that year the first New Canaan High School (now the police headquarters) opened on South Avenue. In 1957 the high school moved into a new building at the corner of South Avenue and Farm Road (now the Saxe Middle School), a site that after a lively town-wide debate won out over an alternative location on the Bliss property on Oenoke Ridge. In 1971 the high school moved into its present imposing — and not universally admired — gray structure on the nearby Waveny estate, but only after the designs of a world-famous architect, Paul Rudolph of Yale, had been rejected as too extreme.

New public school buildings typically require bond issues. Hudson Stoddard observes that even with a demographic shift toward

~75~

an older populace, there has been surprisingly little grumbling from New Canaan taxpayers over the cost of servicing these school construction debts. Perhaps the town's consistently excellent credit rating, accompanied by comparatively low interest rates, lessens the sting.

Stoddard cites the great Asbestos Crisis of the early 1990's as an illustration of how informed and concerned citizens can play an important part in the bricks-and-mortar decisions of a school system. New federal legislation came into force at that time, requiring the abatement of asbestos, a carcinogenic material much used in the past for the insulation of pipes and ducts. Contractors' cost estimates for asbestos removal at the New Canaan High School boggled the minds of many vocal taxpayers. Among them were some retired professional engineers who joined in a committee to work with Town Hall and the Board of Ed to come up with alternative plans and another evaluation. This concerted effort saved the town some $3 million, he recalls.

THE HIGH SCHOOL CLASS OF 1963

When Hudson Stoddard, as Board of Education chairman, spoke to the high school graduating class in June 1963, he related their school experience to what had been going on in the rest of the world. He pointed out that most of them had been born in 1945 — the year World War II ended and the United Nations was founded. "You were the harbingers of a coming generation of Baby Boomers," he told them. "When your class entered kindergarten, there were 150 of you. But only 56 — about a third — stuck it out all the way through New Canaan public schools and are here tonight. The other 94 of your original classmates did not simply disappear; they went off to other towns and schools from which they are probably graduating this month as you are. The other side of the coin is that of the 193 graduates of New Canaan High this year, almost three-quarters started their schooling elsewhere — in many other states and at least ten foreign countries. Our community is not an island or a cocoon; it is part and parcel of a much, much larger community. We are one dot on the vast educational map of America and the world.

"In 1957, the year you entered junior high," he went on, "the

Soviet Sputnik satellite began orbiting the earth, jolting this country into the space age. It was this startling event as much as anything that led the nation to its first concerted reexamination of its educational goals and standards. During your last six years in our schools you began to learn more, and perhaps to be challenged more, than any of your predecessors. (You may think of this as a mixed blessing, but our intentions were good!)

"Looking ahead, the guidance department tells me that 167 of you — an all-time high of 86% — will pursue further education, up from about 60% ten years ago. You will be attending colleges from New England to the West Coast, from the Midwest to the Deep South. Several of you have been summoned by Uncle Sam for military service, which could take you even farther afield. Three of you — God bless you! — have elected a career in nursing, and one proposes to devote herself to the theater. All of you form an important link in your home town's chain of growth and history."

NEW FORMS OF LEARNING TO SERVE A CHANGING SOCIETY

Betty Quinn notes that New Canaanites, as in the past, still seem determined to provide the best educational opportunities within their means. She writes: "Difficult school issues arising out of present-day cultural social changes are addressed together by educators, town officials, community groups, concerned parents and other individuals — even such unpleasant subjects as drugs, safety, harassment and damage to public property — all in the conviction that the young people who occupy our schools for the greater part of each day, every week for ten months a year, are entitled to the most appropriate policies for their welfare."

Since 1950, she points out, there have been major developments in state and federal law affecting public education. "For example, Connecticut has instituted collective bargaining between certified teachers and local school boards; continuing education is now a state-wide requirement to retain certification, and there is a support program for young teachers known as Beginning Educators Support and Training. On the federal level, Section 504 of the Rehabilitation Act of 1973 prohibits discrimination against persons with disabilities, with special regulations applicable both to students and to school employees.

Special education was introduced in the Education for All Handicapped Children Act of 1975, later amended and renamed the Individuals with Disabilities Education Act of 1990, which mandates 'free appropriate public education' for every child from the age of three afflicted by any of thirteen listed disabilities. New Canaan has an extraordinarily comprehensive program to comply with and implement these legislative mandates, supervised by a system-wide director of special education.

"April 26, 1983, was a landmark day for all educators, with the publication of *A Nation at Risk: The Imperative for Education Reform,* a report of the National Commission for Excellence in Education. A national movement for reform and accountability in American education was underway at last. Since 1985, Connecticut Mastery Tests have been administered to all students in grades 4, 6 and 8, and the Connecticut Academic Performance Test is taken by tenth-graders. Results of these tests permit assessments not only of individual students, but also of classes, schools and school systems. Performance comparisons, published annually, invariably rank New Canaan schools at or near the very top."

Ms. Quinn points to many other innovations in our schools over the past fifty years. Among them: parents acting as chaperons on field trips and at social events; also guiding fundraising projects to provide educational "extras"; enrichment of the curriculum through cooperation with such community resources as the Nature Center, the Historical Society, the Library and the Senior Men's Club; giving student aides supervisory responsibility in the lunchroom and at bus-loading areas.

THE CLASSROOM AT THE MILLENNIUM

From Betty Quinn: "Anyone who has not had an opportunity in recent years to visit a school classroom would be surprised and hopefully pleased with the changes in structure, design and furnishings of today's instructional environment. Faculty and students at all grade levels are trained in the use of the computer and multimedia. Hardware and software are constantly updated, and the library/media specialist is in action all over the building. The 'tools of the trade' appropriate to teaching the 3Rs have disappeared: blackboards, erasers, slide rules, overhead projectors, phonograph records, mimeograph machines and typewriters have been consigned to the department of 'collectibles'!

"Although good teaching is and will always remain a highly personalized art, New Canaan teachers are encouraged to enrich their styles with techniques and strategies already known to be effective. Two important resources are research by neuroscientists on how humans learn, and the development within the teaching profession of instructional approaches that foster and enrich learning at different points of growth and development.

"In our schools the roles of teacher, student and librarian have changed dramatically. The library/media center has become the hub of educational activity. With state-of-the-art technologies in most classrooms, a team of students, subject-area teachers, and the library/media specialist can be found working together on a problem-solving assignment integrated across disciplines. The teacher is now a facilitator for learning rather than an agent for dispensing facts; students are no longer passive, sometimes docile, recipients of information, but active participants in a problem-solving activity. Higher-level thinking skills have superseded the memorizing routines of former years.

"Activities are often planned collaboratively to promote interaction among all participants, who learn (individually and as a team) to identify a problem, to gather data from multiple sources, analyze, synthesize, evaluate the data, and communicate the result. In one process called 'cooperative learning', the teacher may form groups of students, usually no more than six to a group, randomly or with a common identity, to deal with a stated problem. Each member of the group is given a role and is responsible for his or her participation. While the groups are at work, the teacher moves among them, assessing and recording the participation level of each student.

"Cooperative learning and various resource-based techniques are designed to equip students to be informed not only about their own community, but to connect effectively with our rapidly changing society. These skills are building-blocks for education 'beyond the walls,' reminding teachers to focus on the process as well as the substantive product. The performance of educators in our schools is constantly subject to review, including reports to the Board of

Education on all areas of instruction at every grade level. Support for teachers, under the direction of the assistant superintendent of instruction, is available through in-service programs, faculty meetings, workshops, conferences and other professional activities. The maintenance of a first-rate, world-class system of public education is a demanding task!"

Looking Ahead — There's No Standing Still

Do our veterans have crystal balls? Let's put them to the test:

Hudson Stoddard: "Two-job households seem to be becoming the norm in New Canaan and across the country, while at the same time the value of early childhood education is increasingly recognized. Today virtually all three- and four-year olds in New Canaan spend time in day-care or pre-schools, giving them an opportunity to make a healthy transition to kindergarten. So far, these facilities and their staffing have been privately funded and operated, but I suspect it will not be long before pre-school in New Canaan will be integrated into the public education system, as has already happened in other progressive communities."

And some provocative speculation by Betty Quinn:

"How does one define a 'school'? Will it continue to be in a building at some convenient location in town? Or will evolving technology permit students to participate routinely from home in assigned educational projects? Can air-conditioned buildings be used effectively in July and August, allowing for flexible programming over the entire year?

"As the training of professional educators encompasses more and more of the new information technology and its related skills, will school boards come under increasing pressure to match salary expectations in other fields? Might private companies — especially high-tech ones — consider establishing their own educational centers for children of employees in communities where the students live?"

THE LONG VIEW OF A DEDICATED TEACHER:
"IF WE DIDN'T TAKE THE TIME TO DREAM…"

From Betty Quinn's warm valedictory: "Most of my days in the classroom as a teacher of science occurred during the space age, and the most popular literary form for my students was science fiction. I told them that I, too, enjoyed these books, but I challenged them to become acquainted with literary works, some of them by authors of science fiction, that describe the basic scientific discoveries upon which the fiction writer relies for his tales of imaginary events. I also encouraged them to read scientific journals, in my belief that the potential of the universe, even the small fraction of it discovered to date, is so unbelievable that one wonders if the human brain can deal with any more knowledge. Today, as the Information Age affects almost all of our human activities, I am even more startled by the potential of the universe.

"When I was teaching in the space age, some adults were inclined to dismiss imaginative students as 'adolescent dreamers.' I smile and wonder where we would be if we didn't take the time to dream about what might be. So, with trust in the human potential to keep on gaining more knowledge of the potential of the universe, and with confidence that all of us will try to use that knowledge for the betterment of mankind, I am sure that the story of the next fifty years in education in New Canaan will be another tale worth telling."

Hudson Stoddard spent his commuting days in New York working in publishing and broadcasting. Throughout, he has also been active locally in a variety of civic and community affairs. Betty Quinn served in the New Canaan school system from 1951 until her retirement in 1997, first as a science teacher and later as an administrator. She received many state and national honors, including the Elizabeth Thompson Award for outstanding science teaching. The full text of her article on New Canaan's schools is on file at the Historical Society.

Texture of a Community

The First Presbyterian Church

St. Mark's Church

9 The Spiritual Dimension

with a Memoir by the Rev. T. Guthrie Speers, Jr.

At present nine New Canaan churches regularly publish their weekly schedules in the *Advertiser*. Here they are, with full names as listed there, and in the same order: United Methodist Church; First Presbyterian Church; First Church of Christ, Scientist; St. Michael's Lutheran Church (ELCA); Congregational Church United Church of Christ; St. Aloysius Roman Catholic Church; Church of Jesus Christ of Latter-Day Saints (Mormons), New Canaan Ward; St. Mark's Episcopal Church; and Community Baptist Church. At the beginning of the last half-century there were just six: the Baptist, Christian Science, Congregational, Episcopal, Methodist, and Roman Catholic. They were joined by the Presbyterians in 1956, the Lutherans in 1962, and the Mormons in 1980.

In 1961 leaders of the Board of American Missions of the Augustana Lutheran Church, considering whether to start a new parish here, commissioned a survey of existing New Canaan churches under the auspices of the Connecticut Council of Churches. This careful study provides as authentic a general description of our religious establishments forty years ago as we are likely to find. It noted that according to the U.S. Census, between 1950 and 1960 New Canaan's population grew from 8,001 to 13,466, or 68.3%. Rapid growth was expected to continue. Over the same period public school enrollment rose from 1451 to 2927, or 102%. "Growth is in young families primarily," the study reported. "One might call it an explosion. New Canaan is definitely a 'young' town."

With the help of this study, we can draw a thumbnail sketch of each of the existing churches in 1961-62:

The Presbyterian Church was the latest arrival. It occupied the former Bliss estate on Oenoke Ridge and had no immediate building plans, according to the pastor, the Rev. T. Guthrie Speers, Jr. (But the Presbyterians built a new sanctuary on the same site in 1970).

St. Mark's had just moved to a "magnificent new edifice" on

St. Michael's Lutheran Church

Oenoke Ridge. Its rector was the Rev. Grant A. Morrill. Its historic church on God's Acre was vacant (and was purchased by the Lutherans following the survey).

The Congregational Church, "the historic church of the community" in the center of town, dated from the 1840's. It had a master plan for expansion to include a fellowship hall and more classrooms. The Rev. Loring Chase was senior minister.

St. Aloysius Church (top)

Congregational Church, United Church of Christ (left)

First Church of Christ, Scientist (below)

The Spiritual Dimension

Community Baptist Church (top)
United Methodist Church (below)
Church of Jesus Christ of Latter-Day Saints (lower right)

The Christian Scientists had recently built a new church in the colonial style ("with a golden dome") adjacent to the Congregational.

The Baptist Church, organized in 1922, served New Canaan's substantial black community. Census figures showed that between 1950 and 1960 this community had grown from 227 to 354, a 56% increase. (In 1960 there were only 13 residents of other minority races.)

St. Aloysius was established in 1896, superseding a Catholic mission here. It had recently opened a parochial school. (St. Aloysius has an interesting architectural history, culminating in the 1995 refurbishment of its 1967 sanctuary; see the parish history listed below).

The Methodist Church, with origins in the 18th century, had moved from Main Street into a new building on South Avenue in 1957; its pastor was the Rev. Charles Austin.

Finally, the Talmadge Hill Community Church, located south of the Merritt Parkway just across the Darien town line, was mentioned in passing. The pastor, the Rev. N.P. Giuliano, lived in New Canaan, as did some of the members.

~85~

The Connecticut Council study was able to assemble figures on church and church school membership from five of these churches, as follows:

Church	Church Members			Church School		
	1950	1960	% Increase	1950	1960	% Increase
Baptist	106	107	1	40	42	5
Congregational	732	1411	93	479	652	36
Episcopal	750	1928	157	363	839	131
Methodist	370	686	85	199	413	108
Presbyterian	—	279	—	—	240	—
Totals	1958	4411	125%	1081	2186	102%

The study noted that most of these increases were proportionately greater than the population growth of the town over the same period. Adding in an estimated 3,240 Catholics, 400 Christian Scientists, 200 Jews and 50 New Canaan members of the Talmadge Hill church, it was concluded that 83.5% of New Canaan residents were related to one or another of these religious groups in 1960.

ECUMENISM IN ACTION

The 1962 Connecticut Council of Churches study concluded with an observation showing ecumenical concern: "We are convinced that the total ministry of the total church to the total community is paramount... [This survey] enables us to take as whole a look as possible at our community and seek to relate our understanding of the ministry of Christ to this town of New Canaan." In fact, New Canaan's first recorded ecumenical movement was already in the offing. From the Presbyterian history: "In recognition of the Church's responsibilities to the people of New Canaan, Mr. Speers joined with three other Protestant ministers in 1963 to found the Committee of Christian Concern. Quickly renamed the Committee of Common Concern to broaden membership, this group tackled the problem of racial and economic discrimination, and the Presbyterian Church publicly supported housing for New Canaan's elderly and minority groups. Out of this came the Interchurch Service Committee."

At first the focus of the Interchurch (later changed to

"Interfaith") Service Committee was on improving the quality of housing for New Canaan's elderly — notably and lastingly the New Canaan Inn and the Schoolhouse Apartments. The agenda later expanded to include start-up support for the Waveny Care Center, the New Canaan Ambulance Corps, Meals on Wheels, and other organizations. This successful and valuable coordination of outreach through the churches led to a movement for joint worship services as well. Turning to the Congregational Church of New Canaan history: "On Jan. 23, 1966, New Canaan held its first ecumenical service. With 17 clergymen present and choirs combined, 750 Baptists, Catholics, Congregationalists, Episcopalians, Lutherans and Presbyterians participated in a Sunday afternoon service at St. Mark's."

Guthrie Speers, the Presbyterian pastor from the church's beginnings in 1956 until his retirement in 1992, recalls many other such events. His buoyant enthusiasm shines through in the following memoir, prepared especially for the Society.

New Canaan Churches as I Knew Them
by the Rev. T. Guthrie Speers, Jr.

On Sunday, June 30, 1963, various churches in New Canaan distributed cards to those in their congregations, asking for their signatures. The cards read, "Gathered together in the worship of Almighty God, the Father of all men, we the undersigned reaffirm our Christian belief in the rights and dignity of people regardless of their race, color or creed. As a witness to our faith, we would join with our fellow citizens in striving to do away with racial or religious discrimination especially in the areas of housing, employment and education."

We had not yet learned inclusive language but we were seeking to be inclusive in our churches and in our community. So began an ecumenical effort that involved the clergy and many of the members of most of New Canaan's churches, an effort that would continue throughout the rest of the century, and that would involve us in efforts on behalf of all sorts of people in all sorts of need.

Our first major effort was in terms of the civil rights March on Washington that same summer in August. The *New Canaan Advertiser* reported the week before the March that a special train would be stopping in Stamford that morning at 3:50 AM and that many from New Canaan would be boarding that train, some from the NAACP of New Canaan and some from the Committee of Christian Concern which represented churches of New Canaan, both members and clergy.

The marvelous sense of camaraderie that so marked that whole day began on that train so early in the morning as we were introduced to and learned to sing "We Shall Overcome." In Washington we gathered at the foot of the Washington Monument where we discovered Grant Morrill, the rector of St. Mark's Church, who had had real qualms about coming but then at the last minute had decided to fly down. My father had given me a tin of sardines for the trip, saying that sardines had been a special treat when he had been in the trenches in France in the First World War. I broke out my sardines, and Grant and I shared them together in what really seemed to be Holy Communion. That Communion continued in the march itself as thousands upon thousands of us, black and white, young and old, linked arms and sang, many of us with tears of joy streaming down our faces.

We returned to New Canaan on a tremendous high, determined to bring something of Martin Luther King, Jr.'s dream to pass in our own community. The Committee of Christian Concern, soon to become the Committee of Common Concern so as to be able to include Jewish and other non-Christian friends, sponsored a series of public forums, meeting in one church and then another, and featuring civil rights leaders such as Whitney Young of the Urban League and Roy Wilkins of the NAACP. African-American student teachers from Norfolk State Teachers College in Virginia served internships in New Canaan public schools. Soon some black families would move peacefully into previously all-white neighborhoods, some black teachers would appear in our schools, some black tellers would work in our banks. Slowly we were becoming a more integrated community.

And a more caring community. The Interchurch Service Committee was formed, later to become the Interfaith Service

The Spiritual Dimension

Committee so as again to be more inclusive. Needs of the town were studied, then task forces were formed to help meet those needs. As a result Waveny Care Center was started, moderate cost housing was built, care was provided for the elderly. A teen center was promoted although it took until the end of the century for that center [the Outback] to come into being.

Person-to-Person in Darien was supported by a number of our churches, providing food and clothing to those in need. "Christmas in April" marshaled volunteer carpenters and painters from the churches and community to repair houses of those whose owners could not afford to repair them on their own but who gladly joined forces with the volunteers.

During the Vietnam War there were peace marches led by some in the churches, and Vietnam refugee families were sponsored. A number of church members joined the Coalition for Nuclear Arms Control which was chaired by Stanley Resor and myself.

For many years a wonderfully special group of developmentally disabled young people has met weekly for Special Church. Now the six residents of the new South Avenue Cottage will soon be moving in and are tremendously excited at the prospect.

An ecumenical gathering of clergy for Martin Luther King Day, 1975. From the left: the Revs. Grant A. Morrill (St. Mark's Episcopal); Paul L. Sartario (Methodist); Richard Butler (visiting Presbyterian); Don A. Washington (Baptist); Jon M. Walton (Presbyterian); Bruce E. Schundler (Congregational); Fredrick E. Erson (Lutheran); Gardner Calvin Taylor (guest preacher, Baptist); Charles C. Smith (Congregational); R. David Cox and E. Kyle St. Claire (both St. Mark's). At far right is the Rev. T. Guthrie Speers, Jr.

From the Advertiser, *Jan. 23, 1975.*

The ecumenical spirit in New Canaan has been nourished by joint services of worship. Each Good Friday a large wooden cross is

~89~

carried through the town by members of all the churches with a marvelously mixed procession following, stopping at several places for a brief reading and prayer. The Episcopalians and the Presbyterians and the Congregationalists have a combined service on the Sunday of Memorial Day weekend, with a picnic and band concert following, going from one church to another in succeeding years. The Lutherans and the Community Baptists have had joint Thanksgiving Day services. The Roman Catholics and Presbyterians have exchanged pulpits on occasion. A community-wide Martin Luther King, Jr. Day service is held each year in different churches.

At the end of the last year of the century a menorah was placed on God's Acre in celebration of Chanukah. The Jewish community gathered for a service in which Gary Wilburn, pastor of the Presbyterian Church, took part. Clergy and lay people of New Canaan continue to work together to build an ever more inclusive community.

Guthrie Speers was pastor of the First Presbyterian Church and a community leader for many years. Now living in New Hampshire, he and his wife Susan visit New Canaan often.

Selleck's Corner Chapel, once a Methodist church

SOURCE NOTES:

Several of the local churches have published their own histories:

St. Aloysius Roman Catholic Church, *Our Centennial Celebration, 1896 - 1996.*

Mary Louise King, ed., *The Congregational Church of New Canaan, The United Church of Christ: 250 Years, 1733 - 1983.*

Mary Louise King, *The First Twenty Years: The First Presbyterian Church of New Canaan, 1956 - 1976.* Updated in Brooke Manning-Hinds, ed., *The First Presbyterian Church of New Canaan, 1956 - 1991.*

Kurt O. Linn, *Methodism in New Canaan, 1787 - 1987,* United Methodist Church of New Canaan, Feb. 2001.

John G. Pennypacker, *St. Mark's and Its Forebears: The First 200 Years, 1764 - 1964.* Supplemented by Helene M. Schnurbush and Grant A. Morrill, *The History of St. Mark's Parish, 1964 - 1971,* and Schnurbush, *The History of St. Mark's Parish, 1971 - 1975.* Also David H. Finnie, *Faith, Hope and Architecture: How St. Mark's, New Canaan, Built a New Church, 1955-1961.*

(The Librarian of the Historical Society would be glad to know of local church histories that have not yet come to the Society's attention.)

OTHER SOURCES:

"New Canaan Church Study, 1962," prepared by the Department of Church Planning of the Connecticut Council of Churches, 22 pages mimeographed, Hartford, c. 1962. A similar study, prepared at the time the Presbyterian Church was organized in 1956, has not been located.

New Canaan *Advertiser,* April 22 and 29, 1993 (30th anniversary celebration of Interfaith Service Committee.)

PARTING SHOT — Filming crews wrap up their work on "The Ice Storm" after stirring up what has been the No. 1 topic of conversation in New Canaan over the past couple of weeks. Scenes in Waveny Park today were scheduled to conclude New Canaan's role in the movies. — (Bukovcik Photo)

Cold cash thaws "The Ice Storm"

A glimpse of Kevin Kline or Sigourney Weaver was enough of a reward for most local movie fans.

But the filming of "The Ice Storm," a $15 million project, also had financial ramifications.

Along with a $20,000 "donation" to the Town of New Canaan, Icy Films, Inc., paid for off-duty police officers and shooting rights at the New Canaan train station, New Canaan Library, Waveny Park and several local businesses and residences.

Sources told the Advertiser that Icy Films spent $23,000 for use of Metro-North train cars and operating personnel. Metro-North spokesmen were unavailable for comment at press time.

Icy Films did not pay for use of the train station and parking areas, according to Jack Reidy, assistant rail administrator for the state's Department of Transportation. The film company was responsible for clean-up costs and repair of any damages.

He told the Advertiser that DOT "tries to cooperate with movie groups. We've already worked with three this year and they do generate some revenues in the areas where they are shooting."

Mr. Reidy said he had no knowledge of the $10,000 that James Schamus, co-producer and screenwriter of the movie, said that Icy Films would donate toward refurbishing the station.

Icy Films did donate $1,000 to the New Canaan Library after a one-day outdoor shoot on the lawn there.

"We found them very easy to work with," commented Library Director David Bryant. "They did not disrupt our operations — which was very important. Inside the library, it was business as usual."

Mr. Bryant also reported that Mr. Schamus was arranging to augment New Canaan's collection of film reference material.

Shooting at Waveny Park, which continues tonight and tomorrow night, cost Icy Films $4,500 which goes into the Town's General Fund.

Off-duty police officers hired by Icy Films will be paid a total of $17,000, it was estimated by Town Finance Director Gary Conrad.

Please turn to Page 12—A

10 Ice Storm in a Teacup

E.T.P.

Take One: New Canaan, Saturday morning, early spring, 1996. Elderly townsperson emerges from delicatessen carrying bag of cold cuts, heads for corner pharmacy to pick up prescription. Notices street is empty of traffic. Is approached by young man running at top speed, wearing jeans, T-shirt and pony tail, waving arms wildly, shouting, "Get out of sight! Get out of sight! They're beginning to shoot!" ETP, World War II combat veteran but no hero, quickly takes cover behind parked van, pokes up head but spots no snipers. Instead, spots young, handsome, willowy woman standing on sidewalk across the street. Reminds him vaguely of recent movie in which gorillas being fed and coddled by woman of strikingly similar appearance. Around corner wheels 25-year old classic station wagon which picks up willowy woman and speeds off down East Avenue. Still no gunfire. ETP proceeds to pharmacy, finds it closed for the day. Cut.

The filming of *The Ice Storm*, by noted director Ang Lee and starring Sigourney Weaver and Kevin Kline, had temporarily taken over Main and Elm. It caused the sort of teapot tempest that can absorb and upset a somewhat self-contemplative metropolitan suburb that occasionally thinks of itself as still a country village. Coming almost at the end of the century, it produced a volcano of indignant letters to the local weekly such as had not erupted since Philip Johnson built his Glass House, almost half a century earlier.

The Ice Storm isn't just any movie. It is based on a novel specifically about New Canaan by Rick Moody, then a thirty-something author who had lived here as a boy for a few years in the early 1970s. His creative-writing teacher at Saxe Middle School, Marie O'Neill, remembered him as a "fine student who really participated in the course I taught for the best students in literature and writing." On December 16, 1973, as young Rick was cultivating his muse here, the town was hit and paralyzed for days by the worst ice storm on record in Connecticut. The storm apparently stuck in his mind as a vehicle

(left) The film crew of "The Ice Storm" on location. From the Advertiser, *May 2, 1996.*

for ventilating the bad vibes about the town ("complicated feelings," he called them in an interview) which he had picked up during his sojourn here. And he laid it on thick: with explicit treatment of debauchery, dysfunctional family life, and general social malaise. Not totally without redeeming qualities, perhaps, but not very uplifting either.

This tangy flavor was not lost when Rick Moody's story fell into the hands of Ang Lee and his screenwriter, James Schamus (*The Ice Storm* won the Best Screenplay Award at Cannes in 1997). Even as the film crew was at work, the late Paul Killiam, impresario of many a local dramatic production and a part-time film maker in his own right, unloaded in a long letter to the *Advertiser* under the headline, "Next Station to Sodom and Gomorra?" He denounced the novel as worthless. "I have peeked at the screenplay," he declared, "and it is even trashier. . . [The town] does not deserve to be depicted permanently on film with such an image." Killiam was also concerned about being cheated: "If sets looking like New Canaan were to be processed in Hollywood, the producers' cost would be in the millions."

How had it happened? Who had authorized the filming — at Waveny Park, on busy downtown streets, at the historic railroad station, now bedecked with sprayed-on plastic icicles? The *Advertiser* got vague and conflicting reports. The producers had apparently paid the standard fees for the use of Waveny. Police Chief Erik Dam acknowledged that armed off-duty officers were being permitted to take extra shifts to control traffic, compensated by the film company and subject to its instructions. The Library had received a donation of $1,000 for the use of its lawn. (It was "business as usual" inside, said Library Director David Bryant.) The producers had promised to make "substantial donations" to the Town once the shooting was over — perhaps as much as $20,000 (although the newspaper had trouble confirming either the amount or the payment). The decoration of the station and usurpation of its parking spaces were being worked out with the railroad, which wasn't talking. Nobody was stepping forward to take credit.

The *Advertiser* weighed in editorially on April 18. The issue was not the content of the film, however seamy: that was protected by the First Amendment. The point was that various public facilities in the town had been turned over rather casually to an outside profit-making enterprise, to the considerable disruption of commerce and the flow of town traffic. "There's been a kind of arrogance that seems to say people here ought to stand in awe of the mighty movie moguls... We ought to be at least aware of what a guest is up to before we invite him in." The paper called for new regulations to curb such sloppy administrative work in future. (The feelings were evidently mutual: in his introduction to the filming script, published in book form in 1997, James Schamus wrote: "One supposes that the reason people spend as much as they do to live in wealthy hamlets [sic!] like New Canaan is precisely so they can avoid things like film crews in their midst.")

Many citizens took a more cheerful view. It isn't every day you get a real close-up of stars like Weaver and Kline doing their stuff. Kids and parents leaned over the fence at the station yard as the cameras rolled. Mike Egerman of Varnum's Pharmacy was interviewed about his own film debut: "I got my fifteen minutes," he said. "They were so accommodating... They made me feel perfectly calm and peaceful." His store was closed for a day so a scene could be shot inside. (Mike is enshrined for Hollywood posterity as "Pharmacist" in the film's cast credits.)

Filming a scene at the Library

Two weeks later, as the film crew was packing up to move on, the *Advertiser* had mellowed somewhat. "Disruption of traffic and confiscation of parking spaces will be dismissed in retrospect as mere inconvenience," the paper predicted. Nevertheless, Town Hall should "get a better handle on such goings-on." People resented "being ordered where and when to go."

The New York Times caught up with the story on May 19 with a big spread on the front of its Connecticut section headed "Lights! Camera! Angst!" First Selectman Lou Moreno conceded to an interviewer that perhaps town officials should have been "more circumspect," and should have provided notice of where filming was going to take place. A reference librarian said that there was a waiting list of 20 to take out Moody's book, which had never received much attention before.

And *Advertiser* editor Ed Chrostowski told the *Times*, "We've had a lot of controversies in town over the years, over fluoridation, budgets and other civic affairs, but nothing quite like this."

Downtown New Canaan after a <u>real</u> ice storm

11 Youth Must Be Served: A Sports Commentary

Don Souden

Usually the flow of history does not respect such calendar conveniences as years, decades or even centuries. But for the story of sports in New Canaan, the midpoint of the twentieth century truly marked both a beginning and an ending. On the one hand, the early part of the 1950s saw the final disappearance of that storied staple of small-town America — the town team. On the other hand, it saw the start of an ever-increasing emphasis in New Canaan on youth sports.

From the end of the Civil War onward, in most of rural America, town pride and emotional well-being were inextricably bound up in the fortunes of the local baseball team. Challenges were regularly issued to neighboring communities, and when a game was arranged, townspeople would gather and root fervently for the local squad. Victory would create a heady euphoria, but defeat could sink the citizens into a deep melancholy — at least until the next game. Things were no different in New Canaan and certainly by the late 1880s we had a town team that would play squads from Ridgefield or Cannondale in games that engaged the attention of everyone. Partisan fervor often ran so high that fisticuffs would break out despite warnings that the constable would be in attendance, and often some fans would have to spend the evening in the local lock-up.

From the turn of the century onward, New Canaan fielded particularly good teams. These early squads were led by John Hersam (whose feeling that the ball scores were not adequately reported caused him to found the *New Canaan Advertiser* in 1908), police chief Otto Schmidt and the first great local pitcher, Hayward "Hy" Davis. For the next couple of decades, New Canaan's town nine won more than 70 percent of its games against top squads from around the northeast, and that success was matched by a hometown basketball team that began playing around 1910.

The Roaring Twenties and the Great Depression

All that changed after World War I, however, as movies and the radio provided newer mediums of entertainment and the automobile conferred a hitherto unimagined mobility. A Sunday spent motoring to the beach or in the countryside proved much more appealing than walking up South Avenue to Fish's Field (where Crystal and Grace streets are today) to watch a baseball game. As a result, by the late 1920s the town baseball and basketball teams were no longer active and local athletes were having to play for teams in Stamford or Bridgeport. The heady excitement of the "Roaring 20s," however, soon yielded to the despair and disillusion of the Great Depression. With so many young men idle and most everyone else looking for inexpensive entertainment, town sports teams entered an era of renaissance. Locally, this saw the emergence of several baseball teams, with the New Canaan Cardinals and later the Maroons the premier squads. There were also town basketball teams and a semi-pro football team. In New Canaan the baseball games were especially enticing because they were free, the result of one of the town's first building booms. Until 1926, most games were played at Fish's Field, but in the fall of that year the property was sold to developers from Stamford. A new sports facility was needed in a hurry, however, because the town's first high school was set to open in January of 1927. As a result, Mead Park (which the Town acquired in 1915, but had rather neglected since then) was hastily improved and a baseball diamond created. And, since it was a public park, admission could not be charged. Instead, a hat was passed and the collection, especially during the Depression years, was always rather meager. Finally, the Depression years of the 1930s saw the first organized athletic programs for the town's youngsters. A regular summer baseball league for youths, with members of the high school varsity serving as coaches, became a fixture and there were also basketball teams organized for both boys and girls. In addition, there were summer day camps and all-sports field days.

War and Post-War

Town teams in baseball and basketball continued to function, though on a reduced schedule, throughout World War II. During those years, the games served less to boost town pride than they did to provide those on the home front with something to take minds off weekly casualty lists and rationing woes. With most of New Canaan's young men scattered around the globe, old-timers came out of retirement to fill out rosters, and sports prodigies like "Jake" Schmitt and Warren Rutledge were recruited as soon as they became teenagers.

The immediate post-war years, however, proved to be the high-water mark for town teams. Those young men who had been lucky enough to return from overseas in one piece sought eagerly to recapture some of their youth and the sports glory they had been cheated out of by the war. In the late 1940s New Canaan supported a semi-pro football team, the Redskins, two basketball teams, the Maroons and the Zebras, and three baseball teams, the Maroons, Zebras and the all-black New Canaan Grays. The Maroons were a continuation of the squad started in the 1930s by the two grand old men of New Canaan sports, W. Bidwell "Pop" Conner and Tom Cronin. As such, they considered themselves the rightful "owners" of the affections of local fans and were not happy to see the formation of the Zebras. That new sports "franchise" was sponsored by Izzy Cohen, the owner of Pierre's restaurant on Elm Street, and was coached by a pair of high school teammates from the 1930s, Julius "Caesar" Groher and Carlton "Pete" Raymond, Jr. Of the third team, the Grays, little record remains. Occasionally, their games rated a few lines in the *Advertiser*, but they mostly toiled in obscurity. It is worth noting, however, that they were accorded the same scheduling access to the Mead Park diamond as were the two all-white squads.

The Maroons and Zebras quickly emerged as heated rivals and, like the Revolutionary War two centuries earlier, often split families because of competing loyalties. Yet, great as the interest was in the various town teams, the end of that phenomenon was already in sight by 1950 and the agent of change was the one-eyed monster television.

By the middle of the century, television was becoming more easily affordable (or readily available at area bars and taverns), and when it came to a choice between watching the Yankees, Giants or Dodgers in relative comfort or going to Mead Park to watch your neighbor play against somebody else's neighbor from a nearby town, the big leaguers won big-time!

The Redskins disbanded first, since football demanded more time and energy than the other sports, but the baseball teams were also gone by 1954. Local basketball teams continued to play, but were forced to play in out-of-town leagues. And with that, the ideal of a "town team" and the focus on the athletic achievements of adults pretty much disappeared forever. As late as 1986 a New Canaan aggregation managed to win the Norwalk recreation department's men's basketball league (albeit with a Norwalk sponsor) and occasional town baseball teams have been formed from time to time only to quickly wither away for lack of interest. But at the same time that the town teams began to disappear for good, the focus of local sports turned increasingly towards the young people. New Canaan fielded its first Little League squads in 1952 and although the local league soon dropped its association with that organization, youth sports programs began to grow by leaps and bounds.

One other event at the midpoint of the century had a profound effect on the course of sports history in New Canaan: Joseph Sikorski was hired as a physical education teacher and coach at New Canaan High School. While attending law school Julius Groher had also been assistant football coach at St. Basil's Prep in Stamford and one of his charges had been Sikorski. Groher had been impressed by the youngster out of Bridgeport and when, years later, he heard that Sikorski was under consideration for a teaching position in town, he put in a good word or three on his former player's behalf. Sikorski was hired for the fall of 1949 and brought with him a new vigor and a host of new ideas that not only revived the high school's moribund football fortunes but started a track program that would eventually enjoy unprecedented success. And with those successes would come the complete transfer of the town's rooting interest from the adults who manned the town teams to the boys (and later the girls as well) who made up the high school's sports teams.

THE GOLDEN FIFTIES

There are those in town who still look back wistfully upon the 1950s as having been a "Golden Age" for New Canaan. However accurate that memory may be for the town as a whole, it is certainly true for the sports program at New Canaan High School. Back then, the high school was among the smallest in the state, yet it managed a series of triumphs that were the envy of much larger communities. In 1950 the baseball team, under the tutelage of long-time coach Loren J. Keyes and led by southpaw hurler Gene Ready, New Canaan won its first — and so far only — state championship. With Sikorski at the helm, the football team won four state championships in the decade. Leading the way were a number of stellar performers, including Ralph Scott, Pete Dauk (the school's first all-state selection), Mark Kelley and the incomparable running back Tony Malizia.

During the same stretch New Canaan High School (which had, at the instigation of Sikorski, officially become the Rams in 1953) won three consecutive state basketball titles. Leading the way was the legendary Maurice "Wilky" Gilmore who set a slew of school and state scoring records, many of which still stand, and was a three-time all-state selection. Heavily recruited, Wilky went to the University of Colorado and helped lead that school to its first NCAA tournament in years.

Wilky was drafted by the professional St. Louis Hawks, but a knee injury prevented him from continuing an athletic career. He had been an honor student and a leader without peer and turned his sights elsewhere. He received a law degree from UConn, returned to town to set up practice and became active in local civic and political affairs. He was elected as a Republican to the Town Council and served several terms before moving to California to become a sports agent. Wilky Gilmore died suddenly in 1993 and his funeral was the occasion for a large gathering of his friends and fans who remembered the young man who first put New Canaan on the national sports map.

Thanks to Sikorski, the 1950s also saw the emergence of another local youngster whose athletic fame would spread across the nation and the entire world, Bill Toomey. Due to Sikorski's efforts, track and field became a major sport at New Canaan High School. From 1954 to 1958 the Rams won a mind-boggling 10 consecutive state track titles and Toomey had been an important part of many of those championships. A protean performer as a Ram (he won medals in a variety of running and jumping events) Toomey turned his attention to the decathlon — a grueling two-day, 10-event test of overall skill — while at the University of Colorado. Bill and his brother Dick (a track standout himself) had followed another outstanding NCHS athlete, Gene Weil, to Colorado. That university's athletic program then got lucky a third time when Wilky Gilmore chose the school because of Weil and the Toomeys. After graduation Toomey pursued his decathlon dream. Despite a series of injuries and setbacks, he managed to set two world records in the event, and in Mexico City in 1968 won the Olympic gold medal for the decathlon. The picture of him crossing the finish line of the last race, both hands flashing a "V for victory" sign, was on the front pages of newspapers around the globe.

One last event of the golden fifties also had important implications for the course of New Canaan sports history: the hiring of Bill Murphy at the high school in 1957 as a physical education teacher and coach. A local boy (he actually grew up in Wilton, but like others from the area at that time he attended New Canaan schools), Murphy joined Sikorski in shaping the destiny of the Rams for

Two of the best New Canaan athletes of the last half-century, Wilky Gilmore (left) and Bill Toomey

decades while also influencing and inspiring several generations of students.

The town itself grew dramatically in the decade and in 1957 a new high school (now Saxe Middle School) was opened on South Avenue. That betokened a change in the Rams' fortunes as well. The football team opened the decade of the 1960s with another state title, and behind the last-second heroics of Gary Liberatore the Rams added another state basketball title in 1962. Alas, that would prove to be the last hoop crown New Canaan High School would earn for the rest of the century. At the same time, a number of new sports were capturing the attention of local athletes. An ice hockey squad was formed in 1957. In 1965 the team finished second in the state cross-country racing, which started about the same time and would earn three state championships in the sixties as well. Soccer became a varsity sport in 1958 as did boys' tennis, while the boys' swim team achieved that status in 1967.

FOOTBALL: ENDURING RIVALRY

For all that, though, the flagship sport at the high school was football. Despite the success Sikorski had achieved, one prize still eluded him — a victory against arch-rival Darien. Until 1927, students from New Canaan and Darien had attended Stamford High School, but both towns were finally forced to build their own schools, giving birth to New Canaan's most enduring rivalry. The promise of many a season, especially in football, was redeemed or destroyed by the result of the Darien game. A last-second triumph in 1931 inspired New Canaan High School music director Lawrence Perry to write the school's fight song, "Onward New Canaan."

But by 1967 New Canaan had not beaten its rival to the south since 1945. One reason for Darien's long win streak was its population growth, which made it much larger than New Canaan at the time. Another was the intense, high-level program installed by its coach, John Maher. Whatever the causes, New Canaan's long victory drought had become a festering sore in the minds of its fans. Even in years when the Rams had good teams, Darien always seemed to find a way to emerge victorious. When New Canaan was less than competitive Darien posted lopsided victories on the order of 70-0 and

64-0. All this would finally change, however, on an afternoon in late September 1967 when the Rams faced Darien at Mead Field.

Change was in the air and on the field that day. The squad was an exciting blend of talented youngsters who had grown up in town (and never seen a New Canaan victory over Darien) and several important transfer students who had never heard of the "Darien Jinx." More important, Bob Lynch had joined the Ram coaching staff from the University of Rhode Island, bringing with him a new offense and a new spirit. The two squads battled evenly throughout the game and with less than a minute remaining the score was deadlocked at 16-16. It was then that the Rams mounted one last drive and with Peil Pennington and Len Paglialunga fueling the offense as they had all afternoon, New Canaan moved to within the shadow of the Darien goal. On the next play, Pennington faked throwing the ball to Paglialunga and instead tossed it to a wide-open Greg Esty in

Coach Joe Sikorski is carried off in triumph after the epochal 1967 victory over Darien

the end zone for a game-winning touchdown. The impossible had finally happened: New Canaan had beaten Darien in football for the first time in more than two decades. Rams fans hugged and kissed each other in disbelief, the players carried Sikorski off the field on their shoulders and the town fathers declared an ad hoc holiday.

Even more, the victory ushered in an era of unprecedented football success in town. Over the next few years New Canaan would win three county conference titles, five state titles and break the state record by recording 33 consecutive victories. The architects of the success were Sikorski and Lynch and many outstanding players like Pennington, Paglialunga, Lem James, Rick Horton, Kurt Horton, Peter Demmerle and Frank Panella. The list could on for pages, but it was an exciting time to be a Ram fan; crowds of more than 8,000 sometimes flocked to Mead Field for important games.

That all came to a clattering halt by the middle of the next decade, but the 1970s saw even greater changes to the sports scene in New Canaan. Hockey began to surpass basketball as the winter sport of choice and a state championship was first brought home in 1972 when the Rams, led by Hank Huidekoper and Jim Tomaselli, toppled Hamden in a stunning upset. Meanwhile, another sport that would soon dominate fan interest in the spring, lacrosse, was started at the high school. In the same decade, there were important changes in the way high school sports were administered. The athletic department was revamped, and what had always been akin to a "mom and pop" operation was put on a more businesslike basis. Moreover, parental involvement was institutionalized by the creation of the Sports Council, an umbrella organization of parents that provided support for all school sports. This would prove to be both a boon and, at times, a problem.

Most significant of all the changes, however, was the rise to prominence of girls sports as a result of federal Title IX regulations that required equal athletic opportunity for women. When New Canaan High School first opened and throughout most of the 1930s girls' teams had commanded a good deal of attention, but for many years thereafter the opportunities were few and girls' teams, if they existed at all, toiled in obscurity. Suddenly, with the force of a federal mandate, girls' sports were put on an equal with footing with boys' sports. The results were spectacular. The girls' tennis and swimming teams were the first to record state titles in the 1970s, but soon New Canaan High School had very competitive teams in all girls' sports and the success of those squads seems to grow every year.

Joe Sikorski retired in 1980 after 31 years at New Canaan High School. In June of that year he was feted to a large farewell dinner, but sadly less than six months later he died of a heart attack while jogging. His death was mourned publicly and as the editorial that week in the Advertiser concluded, "We have lost more than a friend; we have lost a part of ourselves that is irreplaceable." Indeed, Joe Sikorski had been the heart and soul of New Canaan High School for more than three decades, and his memory is still revered by those lucky enough to have known him.

Football: Changing Fortunes

The high school football fortunes went into a steep decline after first Sikorski and then Lynch left the sidelines. Things got so bad that New Canaan lost perhaps the last vestige of its small-town innocence when one losing football coach was hounded out of his job, but his replacement proved no better. By the start of the 1980s New Canaan had lost 27 consecutive games against only a single tie. It was at this nadir that first Vin Iovino and then Lou Marinelli would join the high school faculty and turn the program around.

Iovino was hired in 1980 as the new athletic director. After one more winless season he arranged for Lou Marinelli, against whom he had coached in Westchester County, to become the new football coach. Young, organized and dynamic, Marinelli immediately made the Rams winners and by the next year wrought a near-miracle that once more made the grid Rams state champions. A phoenix had truly risen from the ashes and Marinelli became the winningest football coach in school history. Iovino, meanwhile, continued to direct an ever-burgeoning athletic program at the high school. That program now fields more than two-score sports squads — for both boys and girls — that range from the more traditional activities to crew and gymnastics. The program enjoys the highest student participation levels of any high school in the state.

Youth Must Be Served: A Sports Commentary

In 1950, football, basketball and baseball reigned supreme at New Canaan High School, while girls sports were barely noticeable. Today football still commands the greatest attention, but ice hockey (for both boys and girls) is more popular in the winter than basketball, and in the spring lacrosse (again for boys and girls) has replaced baseball and softball in popularity. And overall, the greatest sports successes of the previous decade — in field hockey, soccer, track and tennis — have been recorded by girls' teams at New Canaan High School. And none of that would have seemed imaginable back in 1950.

The undefeated 1969 New Canaan High School field hockey team that keyed a change in local sports

Outside the Schools

The same growth and change has prevailed in local sports outside the high school. What started as a local Little League franchise in 1952 changed first into New Canaan Boys Baseball and now just New Canaan Baseball, Inc. In the year 2000 nearly 800 local boys and girls participated in seven leagues that embraced more than 65 teams. A Pop Warner football program for youngsters, started in the mid-60s, continues to grow in popularity. The same holds true for all the other youth sports organizations that field a myriad of squads in lacrosse, soccer, wrestling, basketball, field hockey and ice hockey. The key to each program's success is always the high level of participation by parents. New Canaan parents, who care greatly for their children, seem willing to do whatever is necessary to ensure their progeny have the very best of everything. Perhaps nothing so typifies that as the many athletic opportunities they now provide for the town's youngsters.

This spirit was never so amply proved as by the building of a new football stadium at the high school in 1997. Many in town thought that Mead Field, adjacent to Saxe, which had served the town well since 1960, was a showcase sports arena, especially for afternoon football games when the maple trees surrounding it were at their peak of fall foliage. Some residents, however, who had grown up in other areas of the country, thought differently: for them, football meant Friday night action under the lights. Thus the stage was set for a cultural clash when plans were announced to install lights at Mead Field. The town was split, and after much wrangling it was decided to build a new stadium on the high school campus across South Avenue from Mead Field. Moreover, it was decided the new field would be covered with artificial turf so as to provide an all-weather surface that would help alleviate a perceived need for additional athletic space for the town's youth sports programs. The new field was built at a cost of $2.5 million, with all the money raised from private donors. The biggest contributors were Jim Dunning and Rodney Hawes, hence the new stadium's rather unwieldy official title "Dunning Field at Hawes Plaza." By whatever name, however, the field is both an architectural marvel and a pointed example of how important youth sports have become in New Canaan in the past 50 years.

The Strider Invitational

One story that must be told is that of the 4-F Striders track team. Started almost on a dare, the club turned New Canaan into an unlikely but important center of national track and field activity throughout most of the 1960s. The club was started by a group of New Canaan youngsters who decided to enter the state AAU championship meet in 1960. They pooled allowances and otherwise scraped together the money to register their organization and headed to the meet in New Britain one July afternoon. Making the initial journey were Kent Barker, Ted Benedict, Bob Herman, Jacques

Youth Must Be Served: A Sports Commentary

Lebel, Tom Morrow, Marty Mull, Dick Seale and Sandy Souden. Somehow, they captured third place in the entire state and after that there was no stopping them.

They were all teenagers at a time when none of them were of legal age, but they managed enough "smoke and mirrors" legal sleight-of-hand to not only make the Striders a track powerhouse throughout the northeast, but starting in 1961 they began hosting an annual invitational meet in town. For 10 years the Strider Invitational drew the cream of national and international track talent to New Canaan's woeful, sandy, beach-like running facility. Over the course of the decade, the Strider meet attracted nearly three dozen Olympians from eleven different nations and more than 20 world record holders competed. The New Canaan connection was severed in 1970 when all the original Striders had moved on to college and careers, but while it lasted it was something quite unique. Just why so many stellar performers came to town to compete remains puzzling, but perhaps one-time Olympic team javelin thrower Milt Sonsky provided part of the answer. Asked once if he liked coming to compete here because of New Canaan's country ambience, he answered with a thick Bronx accent: "Country? Scarsdale's the country — this is the sticks!" Whatever, throughout the 1960s they came.

Action from the first Strider Invitational; Judge Stanley P. Mead is at the finish line in a baseball cap

Recreational sports have undergone vast changes in the past half-century. The men's softball league sponsored by the recreation department is the longest running sports program in town. It was started in 1932 and has since weathered a depression, several wars and changing personal tastes to remain a summer staple. A women's league began in 1980 (after the men's league's perennial powerhouse Chicken Street put a woman in the lineup for the first — and only — time), but after some success it was terminated in 2000 for lack of interest. A men's basketball league has also endured the past 50 years, but otherwise the department's focus reflects that of the town as a whole by concentrating largely on athletic programs for youngsters.

Another long-running town sports program, the annual Labor Day tennis tournament, has fallen on hard times. New Canaan was once very much a tennis town, and for years the backyard status symbol of choice was a tennis court rather than a swimming pool. The Labor Day tournament was the most talked about athletic event in town. Throughout the 1960s and early 1970s parking spots within a mile of Mead Park were impossible to find on tournament weekend and it seemed half the town was at the courts. That is no longer true; entries are down to a handful and if half the town is still there to watch, they are all disguised as empty space. Why this is so today remains a mystery, but the consensus is that tastes in recreational sports are cyclical and tennis is simply suffering a downturn for now.

Golf would seem to be more popular at the moment, but the Country Club remains the only links facility in town. Several attempts to build other golf courses in New Canaan (at Waveny Park and on two separate parcels of land off Ponus Ridge) have been turned down. Swimming is also popular. Private facilities like the Field Club and the Lake Club were built early in the latter half of the century and there are now plans to build a large, public pool facility at Waveny. During the winter months, the Winter Club off Frogtown Road is a popular venue and provides hockey, figure skating and recreational skating opportunities for members of all ages. Jogging remains a popular recreational activity for many residents, both on the special trails at Waveny and on streets and lanes throughout town. Paddle tennis had a big vogue in the 1970s and the courts at Waveny are still in frequent use all winter. There was even a short-lived flurry of croquet activity in town in the 1960s, but the suspicion persists that was more publicity-driven than a genuine manifestation of interest in that most sedate of lawn sports.

For well over a century sports has been a major thread running through the ever-mutable fabric of our community and continuous interest in local sports has mirrored trends within town. For the people of New Canaan, town pride has always been closely connected with the success of local sports teams. In the early part of the century, townspeople would march en masse to watch a town team while singing "New Canaan Will Shine Tonight", not just with hope in their hearts but with a long nurtured expectation of success.

As the twentieth century drew to a close, local fans were more likely to be singing "Onward New Canaan" while increasingly investing their rooting interest in the fortune of the town's younger athletes. What has remained constant, however, is the enormous amount of town pride in its athletic teams — and the overwhelming success of those teams. New Canaan may still be a small town at the end of a rail spur, but the prowess of its athletic teams has always been the envy of much larger cities on the main line and an ever-enduring source of immense local pride.

Don Souden, who was brought up in New Canaan, is a freelance journalist with a special interest in local sports history. Parts of this article are adapted from his new book, Onward New Canaan!, *which will be available shortly.*

Texture of a Community

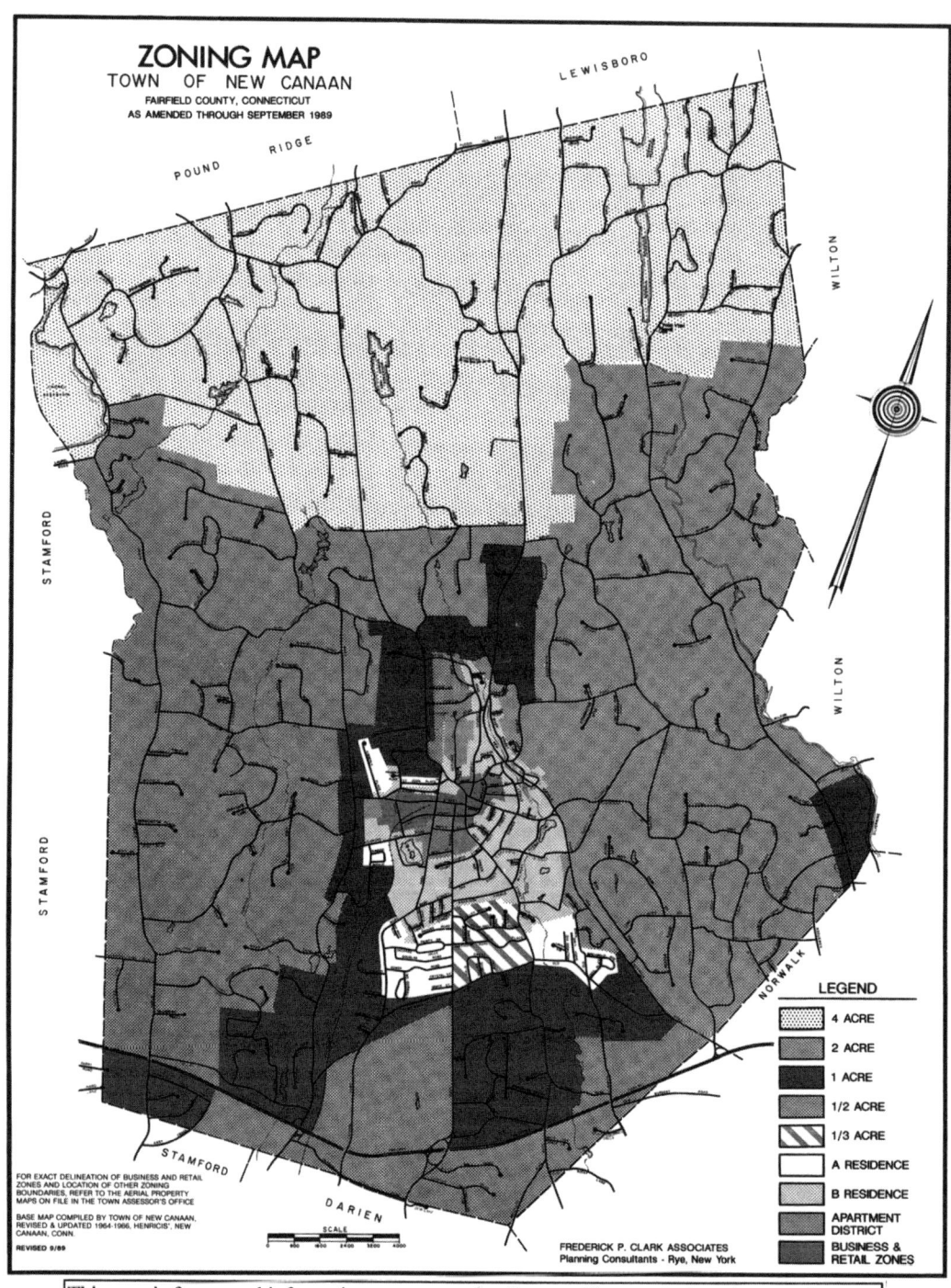

This map is for general information purposes only. For specific zone designation questions see the OFFICIAL ZONING MAP on file in the Planning and Zoning Office.

12 The Celebrated Case of John Senior, Junior

The Editor

> *"The maximum possible enrichment of developers is not a controlling purpose of zoning."*
>
> — *Connecticut Supreme Court of Errors, 1959*

How often does a quiet, peace-loving suburban town need to go to the Supreme Court of the United States to defend its rights? In the case of New Canaan, so far only once.

In the mid-1950s, John L. Senior, Jr. was the owner of 436 acres in the "Lost District" area near the Laurel Reservoir, which at that time was part of the two-acre residential zone. While his application to subdivide was pending before the Zoning Commission (as P&Z was then called), the commission voted to change the existing regulations applicable to some 4000 acres covering the entire northern third of the town, including the Senior property, raising the minimum lot size to four acres. If that decision applied to his land, he would be able to offer for sale only about half as many building lots as he had previously thought he might, and he considered that he had been singularly ill-treated. John Senior's appeal of the Zoning Commission's action was sustained in the Court of Common Pleas. New Canaan in turn appealed to the Connecticut Supreme Court, which in June 1959 reversed in favor of the Town. (146 Conn 531).

Associate Justice King, the author of the unanimous opinion of the state's highest court, described the area in bucolic terms: "heavily wooded, hilly. . . a semi-rural area of natural beauty. . . unspoiled. . . has neither water nor sewer services." He indicated that Senior's argument was essentially that he had been treated shabbily, that "the action of the commission in upgrading the area was unreasonable, arbitrary and illegal." The judge seemed frankly surprised that Senior had "succeeded in persuading the court below" by this line of argument; his burden as plaintiff had been to prove that the commission's action amounted to an illegal abuse of its power, and it was obvious that the commission had acted quite properly under state statutory guidelines. And the judge added rather acidly: "Even if plaintiff proved himself correct in his opinion that he could obtain a larger return from the sale of two-acre lots than from the sale of four-acre lots, . . . the maximum possible enrichment of developers is not a controlling purpose of zoning." The lower court judgment was accordingly reversed. John Senior appealed to the United States Supreme Court, where on May 31, 1960 his case was turned down summarily for want of a substantial federal question (363 US 143). Four-acre zoning was now firmly part of the New Canaan landscape. The town is still batting 1.000 in the Supreme Court.

According to the *New York Times*, which had been following the case through the courts, the outcome of the John Senior litigation was greeted with relief in neighboring towns such as Greenwich and Wilton. The case is apparently still controlling law in Connecticut and has been cited with approval in other states.

Soon after the case was rejected by the U.S. Supreme Court, the Senior marriage broke up, but this apparently was not a matter of *post hoc, propter hoc* (lawyers' quaint shorthand for the childish notion that because A happened after B, it must have been caused by B). In fact his ex-wife, after her remarriage, was heard to say that the injustice of four-acre zoning was about the only thing she and her former husband were really in agreement on.

13   Writers: Our Flourishing Literary Scene

Lester Brooks

In the latter half of the 20th century our town was home, haven or both to increasing numbers of writers. Among them were "perennials" who appreciated the quiet, unhurried pace and New England charm of the town and its easy access to publishers in New York. Maxwell Perkins, the celebrated editor of even more widely celebrated authors (including Hemingway, Fitzgerald and Thomas Wolfe) lived here for many years and there was a literary circle that included William Rose Benet and his wife Elinor Wylie and Padraic and Mary Colum. Many authors came to know New Canaan through visits with Perkins. All in all, some authors were born here, some came for only a while, some stayed and others continued here for a while then moved on.

However it came about, the town numbered hundreds of writers among residents who lived here some time during the last half century. Books still were the predominant medium they used, but the written word has been but one of the ways our authors have reached their audiences. Some have prospered in radio, movies and/or television, as well as through their books or other printed media. The variety of subject matter our authors have chosen is extraordinary, as you will find when you read the notes about our town writers and what they were writing during the last five decades.

NON-FICTION

Some of the older "perennials" used the Melba Inn as their "studio" on a more or less regular basis. Among them was Van Wyck Brooks, distinguished author, steeped in honors and encomiums for his many books about American writers, especially his *The Flowering of New England* (which won him a Pulitzer and national fame) and other highly acclaimed works. (Brooks and Maxwell Perkins were great friends and every Sunday for years they enjoyed long walks together around New Canaan.) Others were Padraic Colum (his books and poetry won him the Irish Academy of Letters Gregory Medal) and his wife Mary (poetry editor of the *New York Times Book*

Review, author of *Our Friend James Joyce* and others); and Martha Foley, editor of *Best American Short Stories* published annually from 1941 to 1967.

Counted among New Canaan's long-term resident writers have been two generations of Prescotts. Orville, (a.k.a. "Bill"), long-time *New York Times* literary critic, wrote *History as Literature*, *Princes of the Renaissance* and many other books, as well as *In My Opinion: an Inquiry into the Contemporary Novel*. He edited many books of short stories, history, prose and poetry and a *Crossroads of World History* educational series.

Orville's son Peter followed his father's path as a literary critic for *Newsweek Magazine*, edited the *Norton Book of American Short Stories*, and wrote *Soundings: Encounters with Contemporary Books*, his study of a boys' prep school: *A World of Our Own*, and *Child Savers: Juvenile Justice Observed*.

Peter's wife, Barnard professor Ann Lake Prescott, wrote *French Poets & the English Renaissance, Imagining Rabelais in England* and *Female & Male Voices in Early Modern England*. Both Ann's brother Anthony and their mother Eleanor have been writers. Eleanor wrote articles for *Reader's Digest* and was managing editor of *Reader's Digest Condensed Books* for many years. Anthony Lake was National Security Adviser in the Clinton years and wrote about international affairs: *The Tar Baby Option* (about South Africa), *Somosa Falling* about the end of that Nicaraguan dictator, and *Six Nightmares*, about U.S. international relations at the end of the century.

History was a field that attracted many other local authors. Among them was Ralph Andrist who wrote books in the *American Heritage* series: *Making of a Nation, History of a Nation, The Confident Years, The 20's and 30's* and *100 Years of Changing Lifestyles in America*. Ralph won a Peabody Award for his radio documentary series on juvenile delinquency and was widely praised for *The Long Death: The Last Days of the Plains Indians*.

William Attwood's wide-ranging career included writing for the *International Herald Tribune, Look Magazine*, and presidential candidates Adlai Stevenson and John F. Kennedy. He was president and publisher of *Newsday* when it won a New York Newspaper Guild's

Orville ("Bill") Prescott

Page One Award. His *The Reds & The Blacks* and *The Twilight Struggle: Tales of the Cold War* were based on his experiences as U.S. ambassador both to Guinea and to Kenya. In another mood he wrote the light-hearted *Decline of the American Male* and *Making it through Middle Age*. The annual Attwood Lectures at the New Canaan Library are named after him.

Beatrice Pitney Lamb was well known in town for her activities with the League of Women Voters and other organizations. Her many writings over the years included *The United Nations*, co-authored with Allen W. Dulles, but it was her deep interest and study of India that resulted in three books on that country and one on *The Nehrus of India*.

David Finnie wrote *Pioneers East: The Early American Experience in the Middle East* and *Desert Enterprise: The Middle East Oil Industry in Its Local Environment*, and about the Gulf War in *Shifting Lines in the Sand: Kuwait's Elusive Frontier with Iraq*. He also penned *The Joyful World of Harry Caesar*, New Canaan's own sculptor in residence.

Historians Polly Schoyer Brooks and Nancy Zinsser Walworth teamed up to write *When the World Was Rome*, *World of Walls: The Middle Ages in Western Europe*, and *The World Awakes: Renaissance in Western Europe*. Polly followed these with her books *Queen Eleanor* (of Acquitaine), *Cleopatra* and *Joan of Arc*, and Nancy wrote *Constantine* and *Augustus Caesar* for the *World Leaders Past & Present* series.

Columbia University professor Howard Schless was the author of *A Poem on Affairs of State, 1660-1714* and another, *A Poem on Affairs of State, 1682-1685*. He also wrote *Chaucer & Dante: A Revaluation* and a book of his own work entitled simply *Poems*.

New York Times' dance critic Walter Terry wrote about the art of ballet and its stars, beginning with *Star Performances* followed by *Ballet Companion, Dance in America* and spotlight celebrity books such as his *Isadora Duncan* biography.

Prolific author Clifton Fadiman was most widely known as one of the experts on the "Information Please" quiz program on both radio and TV in the 1940's. It was a prototype that transmogrified into such modern programs as "Who Wants to Be a Millionaire?" and other excesses that would have horrified Fadiman. He was also a busy editor, translated books by Nietzche, among others, wrote children's books about Ulysses, Hercules and King Arthur, penned books of essays and literary criticism plus light works of collected anecdotes, a playful treatment of *"Mathematica,"* and books about buying and enjoying wine.

Vance Packard illuminated aspects of the American way of life that few had imagined. His *The Hidden Persuaders* explored the use of psychological techniques to sell products and made him an internationally known social critic. He followed this with *The Status Seekers, The Waste Makers, The Pyramid Climbers, The Naked Society, The Sexual Wilderness* and several more, each analyzing a facet of the constantly changing American ways of living.

Homo sapiens basics were dealt with by Robert and Nancy Kolodny in their books. Robert was a co-author of *Human Sexuality* and *A Textbook on Sexual Medicine*, both written jointly with Drs. Masters and Johnson. The Kolodnys collaborated on *How to Survive Your Adolescent's Adolescence*.

Ogden Tanner specializes in nature and habitat. He has written about bears (and other carnivores), beavers (and other pond denizens), and "Animal Defenses" for the television series "Wild, Wild World of Animals" and the books which followed. Wearing his gardening hat, he wrote the *New York Botanical Garden* book, *Garden Rooms, New England Wilds*, then *Urban Wilds, Living Fences, Gardens of the Hudson River Valley* and *Gardening America*. In contrast he wrote *The Ranchers* and *The Canadians* as well as *The Pfizer Story, 25 Years of Innovation*, and *Barnes: An American Story* came from his pen.

Norman Cousins began his distinguished career as a book critic and became the long-time editor of *Saturday Review* magazine, in addition to his activities in education, founding United World Federalists, speaking and writing. He wrote biographies of Albert Schweizer, Nehru and Gandhi, many books about the Founding Fathers, power, immortality and his personal experience, *Anatomy of an Illness*, about how laughter helped him overcome a debilitating disease.

Naturalist John Terres was editor of *Audubon Magazine*, editor of Lippincott's nature books and *The Audubon Nature Encyclopedia*. His own books included *Songbirds in Your Garden, The Walking Adventures of*

Vance Packard

Norman Cousins

a Naturalist and *The Audubon Society Encyclopedia of North American Birds* in 1980.

Sharing her love of flowers, Helen Van Pelt Wilson made them her specialty in *Successful Gardening in the Shade, The Fragrant Year* and *Helen Van Pelt Wilson's African Violet Book.*

Food and travel are the main subjects of many magazine and newspaper articles and books by Patricia Brooks. Among the thirteen books she has co-authored is *The Presidents' Cookbook*. She also has written eleven other books, including *Meals That Can Wait*, a children's book about the Philippines and a series of annual *Connecticut's Best Dining & Wining* books based on her decades of restaurant reviewing for *The New York Times*. In collaboration with her husband Lester, she has written guide books to Britain, Spain, Portugal and New York state and city, and co-authored and edited other guidebooks about New York City, New England and Spain.

Lester Brooks's book *Great Civilizations of Ancient Africa* was a Library of Congress "Best Books of the Year" choice. He wrote *Behind Japan's Surrender, Blacks in the City* (the first history of the National Urban League), and ghosted the influential *To Be Equal*, for the League's president, Whitney Young, Jr., among his sixteen books and many magazine newspaper articles.

Longtime *Scientific American* staff writer John Horgan's first book was *The End of Science*, a dim view of *"...the Twilight of the Scientific Age,"* in 1995. He changed his focus four years later for his book *The Undiscovered Mind*.

Gertrude Schaffner Goldberg, a professor of Social Policy at Adelphi University's School of Social Work, has written and co-written books in her field. Among them: *The Feminization of Poverty* and *Jobs for All*.

Melanie Barnard's specialties are food and cooking, which she has reported in her reviews of area restaurants for more than twenty years for the *Stamford Advocate*. She has also written many cookbooks, including *Short & Sweet* (about desserts) and *The American Medical Association Family Cookbook*.

Edward Hoagland spent his early years in New Canaan and *Cat*

Man, his first book, published before his graduation from Harvard, won him a Houghton Mifflin literary fellowship. Though he has written several books of fiction, he is best known for his many books, essays and articles about travel, exploration and animals. Among these, his books *Walking the Dead Diamond River* and *African Calliope: A Journey to the Sudan* are best known. He edited *The Penguin Nature Library's* 29 volumes from 1985 to 1997 and received Guggenheim fellowships and an O. Henry Award, among many, for his writings.

FICTION

Faith Baldwin was the prodigious doyenne of romance novelists and produced an avalanche of more than 100 books of this popular type, beginning with *Mavis of Green Hill* in 1921 and continuing through 1977. Her lengthy career included writing a regular column, stories and articles for magazines and a dozen movies (beginning with *Week-End Marriage* in 1932, ending with *Queen for a Day* in 1951). She also was one of the founders of the Famous Writers' School. Fable Farm Road's name comes from one of her stories.

Another prolific and widely-known novelist was A.J. Cronin, the successful Scottish doctor who came to the U.S. in 1931, turned to writing and was the author of many international best sellers. *The Stars Look Down*, *The Keys of the Kingdom* and *The Citadel* were among his popular books that later became movies also. Cronin considered *A Song of Sixpence* his best.

Michael Crichton is as widely known for his films and TV series as for his books. New Canaan claims him, though he was born in Chicago, because he lived here with his parents and siblings before moving on for education as a doctor and a career as prolific writer and film and television director. His novels and films brought new terms into everyday use, such as *Andromeda Strain, Terminal Man* and *Jurassic Park*. He created the hospital series "ER" on NBC-TV. Crichton has written about historical events, too, in his *Great Train Robbery, Five Patients* (explaining "the hospital"), and the contemporary world in *Electronic Life* about living with computers.

Another New Canaanite with prodigious output is William Woolfolk who often also uses the pseudonym Winston Lyon. He has written for the CBS-TV series "The Defenders," done novelizations of two Batman shows and was nominated for Emmy Awards for his "A Book for Burning" and "All the Silent Voices." His first book was *The Naked Hunter* in 1953, and he has written more than a dozen novels since, including two, *The Overlords* and *The President's Doctor*, about attempts to take over the U.S. government. He co-authored with his wife Joanna a non-fiction book about *The Great American Birth Rite* and collaborated with his daughter Donna Woolfolk Cross on *Daddy's Little Girl: The Unspoken Bargain Between Fathers and Their Daughters*.

Gerald Green is perhaps best known for the social conscience that infuses his books, award-winning films and TV teleplays. Many of his books have dealt dramatically with hate, and his heralded 1978 TV mini-series *Holocaust* was also a best-seller when transposed to book form. His novel *The Last Angry Man* was a critical and popular success, and he also scripted the movie version. Green's other works include *To Brooklyn, With Love* and *The Chains, Karpov's Brain, The Sword & the Sun* (about Spanish civil wars in Peru), and his skewering of meretricious journalism in *The Heartless Light*.

Allan Sloane has excelled in dramatizing life in his works for TV. His *Bring on the Angels* won accolades and was included as one of the *Prize Plays of TV & Radio, 1956*. Another, highly praised, was his *Teacher, Teacher* in 1972.

Hallie Burnett, with her husband Whit, edited *Story Magazine* for nearly 30 years. She meanwhile wrote the novels *A Woman in Possession* and *The Watch on the Wall*, plus short stories, and co-edited *Story: The Fiction of the Forties*, and other books.

Kelley Roos (the pseudonym for Audrey Kelley Roos) and her husband William, jointly wrote murder mysteries and suspense novels notable for wit and sophistication. Several were adapted for film, including "Come Dance with Me!" starring Brigitte Bardot, and "Scent of Mystery" with Peter Lorre and Elizabeth Taylor.

Robert Daley is perhaps best known for his "tough cop" novels such as *To Kill a Cop, Prince of the City* and *Man with a Gun*, which draw on his past experience as Deputy Commissioner of New York's Police Department. Many of his books have been made into films or TV productions.

Mary Kennedy who acted on Broadway and in early films, wrote plays, poetry and books on a wide range of topics. Her poetry won awards from *Saturday Review*, the Poetry Society of America and the New York Women Poets for such lyrical works as *Ride into Morning, Behind the Day* and *The Bourrichon*.

Guyana native E.R. Braithwaite's best known novel, *To Sir with Love*, told of his experience teaching unruly white students. It won a *Saturday Review* award and became a popular movie. His other books include *Paid Servant, Reluctant Neighbors* and *Honorary White*.

Cultural New Canaan and its surroundings interested several writers. Laura Hobson's *Gentleman's Agreement* portrayed anti-Semitism in full flower. She wrote several more books attacking bigotry. Sloan Wilson's *The Man in the Gray Flannel Suit*, depicted commuter life at the half-century mark. He followed through with a sequel nearly thirty years later (*The Man in the Gray Flannel Suit II*), having written ten other books in between. Yet another view was supplied by Rick Moody, who lived here briefly in his high school years. His 1994 novel *The Ice Storm* gave a decidedly dim picture of life in New Canaan. All three of these books reached still larger audiences in their film versions.

Winner of the Flannery O'Connor Short Story Award in 1999, William Roorbach, who grew up in New Canaan, has written for the *Atlantic* and *Harper's* and teaches creative writing at Ohio State University. He is the author of *Summers with Juliet* and *Writing Life Stories*.

BOOKS FOR CHILDREN

The success of *Red Head*, about his young son, brought Edward Eager and his family to Silvermine Road in New Canaan. There he wrote children's books about local life in works such as *Mouse Manor* and *Playing Possum*, which critics called a "distinctive contribution" to 20th century children's literature. In another successful series of books he integrated the realism of ordinary living with romantic adventures springing from a "magic" coin or other object in a child's life.

Mary Stolz specialized in young adult novels, children's books and short stories. Her *Belling the Tiger* in 1962 and *The Noonday*

Friends in 1966 were Newbery Award Honor Books, and the American Library Association Notable Book citations went to her *The Seagulls Woke Me, Belling the Tiger*, and *Quentin Corn*.

Armstrong Sperry wrote for children about the exotic places he had traveled, which led to his *Pacific Islands Speaking*, *All about the Jungle*, and *South of Cape Horn*. He wrote action books also, about John Paul Jones and Captain Cook. His *Call It Courage* won a Newbery Medal and *The Rain Forest* received a Boys' Clubs of America Junior Book Award.

Elizabeth Yates focused on juvenile fiction and books for youths. She was early on the race relations scene with *Amos Fortune: Free Man*, and a biography of *Prudence Crandall, Woman of Courage*. Some of her other titles were *Carolina's Courage, Children of the Bible*, and a *Place for Peter*. Her autobiographical book was *Call It Zest: The Vital Ingredient after Seventy*, but she followed it with one for young people called *One Writer's Way*.

SPORTS

One of the foremost sports writers of his day, Walter W. "Red" Smith was widely admired for his incisive reporting, ranging from fishing to football and events such as the Olympics. He wrote frequently for *Saturday Evening Post, Colliers* and *Reader's Digest* in addition to his newspaper columns for which he won a Pulitzer Prize for distinguished commentary. His book on *Fishing Around the World* spoke of one of his interests, and his collected columns in book form were popular, as were *Red Smith's Sports Annual* and *Press Box: Red Smith's Favorite Sports Stories*.

Mike Lupica is known as an on-air sports journalist and commentator at various times for ESPN, WCBS-TV and WNBC Radio as well as his syndicated sports column for the *New York Daily News* and *Esquire*. He has co-written books such as *Reggie: The Autobiography of Reggie Jackson* and *Parcells: Autobiography of the Biggest Giant of Them All*, about football coach Bill Parcells. Mike's *Shooting from the Lip* is a collection of "quips and gripes in the grand tradition of dyspeptic sports writing." He also has written several mysteries featuring his sleuth Peter Finley.

Armin Keteyian has been an editor at *Sports Illustrated* since 1982 and has won prizes for his writing (Grand Prize from *Sporting News* for a Best Sports Stories of the Year, 1983, and others). He has specialized in books about sports figures: *Racquetball: Dave Peck's Championship Racquetball System; Rod Carew's Art & Science of Hitting* (with Carew and Frank Pack); *Calling the Shots* (with Mike Singletary) and *Catfish* (with James "Catfish" Hunter.)

Margaret Cabell Self, who founded the New Canaan Mounted Troop, was a prolific writer about horses and all things equestrian. Her books included "how to" care, handle, ride and enjoy horses from her earliest, *Teaching the Young to Ride*, through *A Horseman's Encyclopedia* and *The Problem Horse and the Problem Horseman*. Her writings ranged from fiction involving horses (*Sky Rocket: The Story of a Little Bay Horse*) to her entries in *Encyclopaedia Britannica* and *Compton's Encyclopedia*. She also was for many years a member of the Norwalk Symphony and San Miguel Chamber Ensemble in Mexico as well as concertmistress of the Block Island Chamber Ensemble.

Another horse lover was Jean Slaughter who raised them and wrote *Horsemanship for Beginners, Pony Care* and *Horses Around the World*. She wrote fiction for young people (*Summer Pony, Gabriel* and *Winter Pony*) as Jean Slaughter Doty, after her marriage to cartoonist Roy Doty.

(There are many, many New Canaan authors whose names are not found in this brief survey. In late 2000, the New Canaan Library published a useful pamphlet, *New Canaan Authors' Corner*, edited by Peter Prescott. It lists some 500 names of local writers and illustrators, many of whose works are to be found on the Library's shelves.)

Lester Brooks is a prolific author, often in collaboration with his wife Patricia. They have produced many books and articles about their extensive travels.

New Canaan authors on display at the Library

Writers: Our Flourishing Literary Scene

This historic house on Park Street was an incubator of some of the finest American fiction of the twentieth century. Once the home of famed Scribners editor Maxwell Perkins, it became the focal point of a distinguished New Canaan literary circle. The house has been restored by the present owners, architect Richard Bergmann and his wife Sandra.

Texture of a Community

14 Visual Artists: A Vivid Panorama

Ann Bridgman, with Ruth Carroll

Over the years New Canaan has attracted more than its share of artists, art critics, and collectors — far more than can be covered in this survey. Among the earlier ones was Van Dearing Perrine, celebrated for his views of the palisades of the Hudson River, who died here in 1955. His daughter Mary lived in the "Pink House" in Silvermine while teaching art at the New Canaan Country School. Also nationally known were his contemporaries Howard Hildebrandt, a portraitist, and D. Putnam Brinley. Jean MacLane, mother of New Canaan architect John Johansen, won awards for her portraits; her work is represented at the Art Institute of Chicago and at the Smithsonian's portrait gallery. Adrian Lamb was known as a portraitist and "recreator" of original paintings by other artists. Jimmy Ernst, who lived on Ponus Ridge, was a prominent formal abstractionist. He was the son of Max Ernst, German surrealist.

Walter DuBois Richards and his wife Glenora have been called the town's "first couple" in the arts. Wally, who will celebrate his 94th birthday this year, has portrayed New Canaan scenes for the last 60 years. His work includes lithography, watercolor and illustrations for magazine and advertising media, as well as thirty-seven U. S. postage stamps. During World War II he served as official historian/painter for the U. S. Air Force. Glenora Richards, a miniaturist, renders her delicate portraits on both ivory and canvas. She designed stamps commemorating poet Edna St. Vincent Millay and Dr. Mary Walker, the Civil War surgeon.

Sculptors

Paul Manship, creator of the "Prometheus" fountain sculpture in Rockeller Center, once lived here. Harry Caesar moved here in 1946, and stayed. In 1974, at the age of 60, he took up sculpture as a hobby and turned it into a successful second career. Harry's work is on display at the Waveny Care Center and in local private collections; his "Alleluia" stands in the courtyard at St. Mark's Church. He is the

(left) Charles Saxon's first New Yorker *cover: New Canaan station at Christmas*

~127~

founder of the New Canaan Sculpture Group which works out of the lower level of the Carriage Barn at Waveny.

RESCUE AND RESTORE

Ginny Rider's curiosity about WPA art was the spark that ignited the Rescue and Restore project. She formed a citizens' committee to locate and restore murals, paintings and sculpture done by New Canaan artists under the Works Progress Administration and the PWAP (Public Works Art Project) during the era of the Great De-pression. (These Federal programs provided funds to support local artists, with communities contributing materials and working space; the community commissioned the artist on the basis of his or her sketches.) Through the efforts of Rescue and Restore several New Canaan art works, previously thought to have been lost or destroyed, have been recovered. Among them are two by Walter Kirby: large depictions of New Canaan, one as of 1834, the other a century later, that have been restored and now hang in the central meeting room at Town Hall. Kirby, who was also an architect, designed the town's fire house. In the same room at Town Hall are five paintings of Mead Park by Ernest Albert, Jr. The Library has several allegorical paintings by Laicita Worden Gregg. George Avison's mural of the Old Meeting House of Canaan Parish in 1825 is in the Historical Society's auditorium. Other local artists involved in WPA projects were Justin Gruelle, Helen Hamilton and Ralph Nelson. Several decorative metal "New Canaan" road signs for posting at the town's borders were forged by Clifton Meek of Silvermine, who had been an animator at the Disney studios. Other WPA sculptors were Katherine Lawson, Robert C. Wakeman and Albert Jacobson, whose plaster bas reliefs are also in Town Hall.

"Family" by Harry Caesar

The aim of Rescue and Restore is to display WPA art, not only for its historic value, but also for its original purpose — to adorn the town's public spaces.

THE SOCIETY FOR THE ARTS

In 1976 a nucleus of artists set about transforming the old carriage barn at Waveny into the Carriage Barn Arts Center. The group was spearheaded by Jan Fenton and Helen Barnes, assisted by a small

Visual Artists: A Vivid Panorama

army of other volunteers, including master carpenter Clifton Webb and architect Dick Bergmann. Thus was born a permanent home for the New Canaan Society for the Arts. The society sponsors several shows every year, including a juried exhibition, a members' show, a photography show and a young people's exhibit, and its gallery is available for other individual and group shows. In 1997 the space was dedicated as the Betty Barker Gallery. Betty, who died earlier that year, was a principal benefactor of the Society and a gifted artist whose paintings hang in many a New Canaan home.

In January 1983 a lively musical show, "To Thee We Sing," was presented at the Carriage Barn. It was based on Mary Louise King's Portrait of New Canaan, published by the Historical Society in 1981. The musical, highlighting major events in the history of the town, was written by Paul Killiam and Hank Miles. Killiam also created a film committee at the Carriage Barn, which presented little-known vintage movies from his vast personal collection.

THE OUTDOOR ART SHOW

The annual New Canaan Outdoor Art Show started in 1955, the brainchild of Jane Faus and a few other artists, supported by the Chamber of Commerce and its president, Frank Thoms. Each fall almost 500 paintings were displayed in shop windows or strung on metal modules designed by Victor Christ-Janer, lining Elm and Main streets and other streets beyond. It was more than an exhibition: it became a genuine folk festival. Ten thousand people came to the first show. Merchants enclosed announcements with their mailings. A four-car "art train" brought visitors from Manhattan; in 1956 (an election year) they were greeted at the station by a GOP mobile canteen dispensing free coffee and doughnuts, while the Democrats manned their own booth further down the street. Viewers were invited to vote for their favorites, but the only prizes were ribbons. Among the popular winners in 1957 were an oil-burner serviceman and an optometrist. That same year the show was written up in *Art News*.

No entry fee, no commissions, no prize money, no profits. A tremendous amount of work for the committee of volunteers. Yet the outdoor art show thrived. In 1959 the exhibition got its first juror,

"But will it fly?" Darius Fisher (right) and Darin Ricco visit a Carriage Barn art show, 1989

~129~

John Gordon, a curator at the Whitney Museum. In 1961, three judges were engaged: Albert Christ-Janer, dean of the art school at Pratt Institute; Albert Dorne, founder and president of the Famous Artists Schools; and Gibson Danes, dean of the Yale School of Art and Architecture. Before long, programs were printed each year bearing a "sunburst" logo designed by John McClelland. Cash awards were introduced to back up the ribbons. Some glitches occurred: one year the works to be displayed were locked in the women's jail in the basement of Town Hall; they had to be released and carried upstairs to be viewed by the judges, then returned to the prison until it came time to hang them.

In short, what began as a small town street show developed into a major art exhibition, with jurors recruited from the Guggenheim, MOMA, and one year the eminent Henry Geldzheler of the Metro-politan Museum. The quality of the work so impressed these professionals that they initiated a new "Jurors' Award" as prize in the amateur class. But some sidewalk critics felt that abstract works were dominating the awards, and the *Advertiser* protested editorially that the "oils, watercolors and pieces of sculpture cannot be deciphered." Once an award-winner complained that his painting — an abstract nude — had been hung upside down. Turning it the other way up revealed the subject matter more clearly, causing embarrassment among the organizers, some of whom were not certain that

In front of Town Hall at the Outdoor Art Show

Visual Artists: A Vivid Panorama

such racy material was *comme il faut* in an open-air show, except possibly in Greenwich Village or on the Left Bank.

In 1972, after too many disappointments and disruptions owing to foul weather, the show moved indoors — first to the high school and later to Waveny House. And as with many other non-profit activities, with more and more housewives joining the work force, it became increasingly difficult to find volunteers to do the time-consuming work involved. The last New Canaan Outdoor Art Show, sponsored now by the Young Women's League of Connecticut, was held at Waveny House in 1988.

The Silvermine Guild

For the Silvermine Guild Center for the Arts, the fifties were banner years. Until then the only building on the Guild's campus had been an old barn housing the "Knocker's Club," the seed group of artists that formed the Guild in the 1920s. In 1950 an entirely new building, Gifford Hall, was dedicated, made possible by a generous gift from Florence Schick Gifford. Six years later a sculpture and ceramics studio was dedicated by sculptor Jacques Lipschitz, augmenting a shed big enough only for a potter's wheel and a kiln. The director of the Guild's art school at the time was Gail Symon, a New Canaan portrait painter; under her direction the Silvermine College of Art was accredited by the state to offer a program leading to an associate in fine arts degree. Although the accreditation program has been discontinued, the school offers year-round instruction for adults and children in all aspects of the visual arts.

The annual juried exhibition, originally the New England Show, expanded and has been renamed Art of the Northeast USA. It is now in its 53rd year. A National Print Show is held biennially. Artist members, now numbering almost 500, display their work individually and in group shows year-round. The guild also offers seminars, workshops and lectures. At the guild's chamber music center, inaugurated in 1959, four or five concerts are performed each summer.

Friends of the Library Art Committee

Since 1957 the Art Committee of the New Canaan Library has been mounting exhibitions at the Library. One of its earliest shows

Silvermine tree logo designed by John Vassos

was a blockbuster exhibition of twentieth-century masters including Jasper Johns, Robert Rauschenberg, Andy Warhol, Helen Frankenthaler, Roy Lichtenstein, Alexander Calder, Joseph Albers, Kenneth Noland, Ad Reinhardt, Raoul Dufy and Georges Rouault — all on loan from New Canaan collectors.

Norman Cousins, the editor of the *Saturday Review* who lived in Silvermine, exhibited photographs he had taken on his world travels; present at the opening was his friend Margaret Bourke-White, who later had her own photography show at the Library. Over the years there have been hundreds of other shows: local artists' depictions of town landmarks; book art; early Americana; children and parents; illustrators; student shows; architectural exhibits; photography; sculpture, furniture and design. A recent show displayed a 50-foot scroll painting of the Battle of Gettysburg, with a teeming cast of 5000, by New Canaan's inimitable artist Brian Kammerer. Most exhibits were mounted in the H. Pelham Curtis Gallery, donated by the Curtis family in 1980.

Illustrators

Our town has been the home of a number of gifted illustrators. In the early days there were George Avison, Albert Harrison, Ernest Albert, Sr. and his son Ernest, and the Gruelles — Justin and Johnny — who lived in Silvermine just over the border. Later figures included Whitman Bailey, Melbourne Brindle, Keith Ward and Arthur Szyk. Brindle, whose work appeared regularly in the Saturday Evening Post and Colliers, contributed several pen and ink drawings to Landmarks of New Canaan, published in 1951 by the Historical Society. He also designed four stamps for the National Trust for Historic Preservation, and his illustrations of early Rolls Royces purr through the coffee-table classic, *Twenty Silver Ghosts*.

While still in his teens, Whitman Bailey studied with Howard Pyle, who discovered that Bailey was color-blind and steered him toward working in black and white. About one hundred of his drawings appeared in the *Advertiser* over the years. Keith Ward, known for his illustration of children's books, also did advertising art and portraits; he created the "Fire Chief" pups for Texaco and the rhinoceros for Armstrong Tires. Noel "Bud" Sickles developed the comic strip

"Scorchy Smith." During World War II he worked on military manuals and later specialized in illustrations for stories about the Civil War, on which he became an expert.

Edwin Eberman was a New Canaan resident for forty-five years. A founder and director of Famous Artists Schools, he wore many other hats. An accomplished watercolorist, he turned to pen and ink to contribute many drawings to *Landmarks of New Canaan*. Ed served on various town boards and commissions, and was one of the founders of the New Canaan Land Conservation Trust. At his home on Hallowe'en, neighborhood kids lined up to have themselves caricatured in their disguises.

The late Ralph Pereida produced ten books of art instruction for the Grumbacher Library and received many awards from the Society of Illustrators. Locally, he designed the sets for the Walter Schalk Dance Reviews, served seven years on the Parks and Recreation Commission, and headed the Waveny Advisory Commi-ttee. He was honored as the Gridiron Club's "fall guy" in 1993.

David Johnson is a young New Canaan illustrator to keep an eye on: his incisive line drawings of authors appear regularly in the *New York Times Book Review* and other publications.

Arthur Szyk, one of the master illustrators of his time, became an American citizen while living in New Canaan. It was said that his searing anti-Nazi political cartoons and caricatures provoked Hitler to place a high price on his head. "Art is not my aim," he once declared; "it is my means." Szyk also produced illuminated manuscripts in a style usually associated with medieval religious art. "Washington and His Times" and "The Declaration of Independence" are among the manuscripts that display his rich coloration techniques. The Historical Society mounted a stunning exhibition of about one hundred of his works in the summer of 2000.

In 1996 former New Canaan artist Ann Mitchell wrote a charming picture book, *Where the Heart Is*, depicting the various places she has called home. The book's color illustrations in a folk art style include the New Canaan train station, God's Acre and the reredos at St. Marks Church.

Texture of a Community

Cartoonists

Fairfield County is said to have more syndicated cartoonists per square mile than any other area in the country, and New Canaan has played its part. John Cassel started the ball rolling in the 1930s as a political cartoonist for the *New York World*. Edwina Dumm, the nation's first full-time female editorial cartoonist, also created a comic strip, "Tippy," for King Features. Another syndicated strip, "All in a Lifetime," was produced by Frank Beck. Paul Arlt drew editorial cartoons for the *New York Herald Tribune* in the 1950s.

Paul Webb's moonshining hillbilly "Mountain Boys" appeared in *Esquire* magazine and elsewhere. Several of Paul's original drawings graced the walls of "Izzy's Place," the popular Elm Street watering hole where he and his cronies lunched each week. Bob Bugg was known as a jack-of-all-drawing-boards artist: his genial good nature and cartooning skills were often called upon to create posters and flyers for one local good cause or another.

Paul Webb's "zebra" mural in Pierre's restaurant; another ad for Izzy's place

Among the New Canaanites represented in the *New Yorker*, the acknowledged pinnacle of the cartooning world, are Helen Hokinson, Dick Cavelli, Tom Henderson, Roy Doty, Virgil Partch and Robert Osborne. Perhaps Charles Saxon caught the town's atmosphere more precisely than any of the others, with deft caricatures of his fellow townspeople going about their business at zoning meetings, at the train station, at cocktail parties, with sly but kindly captions to match. The first of his many *New Yorker* covers, on December 19, 1959, depicted commuters rushing home from the New Canaan station at Christmas time, loaded down with holiday gifts. The magazine's cartoon editor, Lee Lorenz, called Saxon a chronicler of middle-class suburbia with a very sophisticated eye. A 1997 exhibit at the Library's Curtis Gallery, "22 Cartoonists: A Portfolio of Smiles," was dedicated to the memory of Chuck Saxon.

BEHIND THE LENS

Art D'Arazien was renowned for his innovative technique in lighting and color which enabled him to show massive industrial subjects with breathtaking clarity and grandeur. His work appeared on the covers of many a corporate annual report. At age 22 Pedro Guerrero became Frank Lloyd Wright's official documentary photographer in Taliesin West, Wright's vast operation in Arizona. He worked for the master until Wright's death in 1959, twenty years later. His photos are collected in *The Wright Picture: Photos by P. E. Guerrero*.

The work of Ozzie Sweet, who lived here for many years, appeared on the cover of *Newsweek* more often than that of any other photographer. Among those who posed for him were Albert Einstein, Dwight Eisenhower, Yogi Berra, Ingrid Bergman, Pope John Paul II and Ernest Hemingway. Ozzie published eighteen books of nature and wildlife photographs, and he gave illustrated lectures on his travels at the New Canaan Nature Center and elsewhere.

Russ Kinne is another nature photographer and environmentalist who has given exciting slide presentations of photos from his worldwide travels. He has often focused his lens on New Canaan's ponds, meadows and marshes as well. Phoebe Dunn is famous for her winning portraits of children for private clients and commercially, often using New Canaan youngsters as her models. Malcolm Smith, who lived here in the 1960s and 1970s, was a leading architectural photographer. Edward Keating, a New York Times staff photographer who grew up in New Canaan, recently had a showing at the Library of his black and white photos of New York City.

John Bukovcik and Syd Greenberg were both army photographers. Each in his own way has chronicled New Canaan's people and happenings for the past fifty years. Although their work was not limited to the town, their photos have added life and clarity to thousands of *Advertiser* columns. Many of these original photographs and negatives have been donated to the Historical Society.

CRITICS

What would art be without art critics? James Thrall Soby wrote exhibition catalogs for the Museum of Modern Art on artists such as Chirico, Dali, Rouault, Klee, Modigliani, Ives Tanguy, Balthus, Juan Gris and Joan Miro. His book *Modern Art and the New Past* broke new ground in its defense of modern art. Henry LaFarge, a nephew of the noted John LaFarge, was associate editor of *Art News*. In 1956 the *Advertiser* carried his review of the first New Canaan Library Loan Show.

Ann Bridgman lived in New Canaan for thirty-five years. She has done publicity for the Silvermine Guild and was director of the Ridgefield Guild of Artists.

Ruth Ogden Carroll, a New Canaan native, studied with artist Carroll Holliday and served as the assistant to the dean of Silvermine College of Art. She and husband J. Otis Carroll reside in New Canaan where they raised their two sons.

Visual Artists: A Vivid Panorama

"New Canaan isn't _really_ in the country. It only _looks_ like the country."

One of Helen Hokinson's matrons interviews a maid

Texture of a Community

15   A Bow to the Performing Arts

Clockwise from top right: orchestra rehearsal at Smith Hall, Congregational Church; the town band, with Joe Sweet conducting at an Historical Society Ice Cream Social; John Rogers at work on a set for the Town Players; Jonathan Edwards directing a rehearsal for "Peter Pan" at the Town Players; high school girls rehearsing with dancing master Walter Schalk.

Community Orchestra Rehearsal — Walter Richards

~139~

Texture of a Community

NEW CANAAN: COPING WITH ITS "NEW LOOK"

BY ED CHROSTOWSKI

Top: Main Street, part of the "magic circle."
Above: Horses grazing at the town's 300-acre Waveny Park.
Top left: The Firehouse.
Bottom left: The Historical Society.

From Fairfield County, *October, 1981*

16 Related Historical Society Resources

Janet Lindstrom, Executive Director

The New Canaan Historical Society has published *Annuals* on the town's history since 1943. Details on many topics covered in this book can be found in these publications and in the Society's files.

Architecture:

> *New Canaan Modern 1947-1952*, an extract from the 1967 *Annual*
> 1983 Video – "Architects Revisited – New Canaan Architects, 1953-83"
> 1986 *Annual:* Philip Johnson in New Canaan

History:

> *Portrait of New Canaan*, by Mary Louise King, 1981
> *The Making of Main Street*, by Mary Louise King, 1971
> 1971 *Annual:* The Early Years of Fire Companies in New Canaan
> 1973 *Annual:* History of The New Canaan Fire Company No. 1 (part 2)
> 1981 *Annual:* Fires and Fire Fighters in New Canaan, 1845-1881
> The First Hundred Years of the Telephone in New Canaan
> Silliman's 114 years
> New Canaan in Newspapers
> 1982 *Annual:* New Canaan Inns
> 1992-93 *Annual:* Wampum to Wall Street
> 1991 Video – "New Canaan Celebrates"

Physicians:

> 1983 *Annual:* Two Centuries of New Canaan Doctors

Business:

> 1955 *Annual:* The Shoe Industry in New Canaan
> 1959 *Annual:* New Canaan's Oldest Active Businesses
> 1966 *Annual:* New Canaan's Oldest Drug Store (Cody's)
> 1979-80 *Annual:* The History of Hoyt's Nursery (2 articles)
> 1973 *Annual:* New Canaan in Newspapers, 1818-1973

Texture of a Community

Arts:

   1955 *Annual:* Historical Society Art Series in New Canaan

Parks:

   1945-1949 *Annuals:* New Canaan's District Schools
   The Story of Waveny, from the 1969 *Annual*

Schools:

   1998 *Annual:* Early New Canaan Schools

"Skating on Mill Pond"
by Walter DuBois Richards

Index & Credits

A&P, 55
Ackerly, Dana C., 6
Ahearn, Dick, 23
Airdraulics, 17
Albert, Ernest, Jr., 128, 132
Albert, Ernest, Sr., 132
Allen, Yorke, 5, 25, 27
American Legion, 23
Americans with Disabilities Act, 31
Andrist, Ralph, 116
Archbishop of Canterbury, 7
Arlt, Paul, 134
Asie (restaurant), 70
Attwood, William, 116
Auer, William ("Billy"), 68, 69, 70
Austin, Rev. Charles, 85
Avalon Communities, 8, 35, 60
Avison, George, 128, 132

Bach family, 56
Bach, Jack, 23
Bailey, Whitman, 132
Baldwin, Faith, 120
Baldwin, William, 9, 10
Bank of Boston, 59
Bank of New Canaan, 59
Bank of New York, 59
Bank on Main Street (restaurant), 70
Barker, Betty, 129
Barker, Kent, 108
Barnard, Melanie, 119
Barnes, Helen, 128
Barnes, Martha, 52
Batterson, Bob, 35
Beck, Frank, 134
Becker, Margaret, 24
Benedict, Ted , 108
Benet, William Rose, 115
Berg, John, 5
Bergmann, Richard, 40, 41, 125, 129
Bergmann, Sandra, 40, 125
Bertram, Albert, 56
Bertram, Bruce, 56
Bertram, Jake, 56
Bestercy, Brent, 42
Billings, Chester, Jr., 4, 29

Bistro Bonne Nuit, 70
Black, Carl, 52-53
Bliss, Phil and Jeanne, 34
Bliss, Robert L., 3, 25, 27, 28
Blue Water Café, 69, 70
Board of Education, 73
Bogey's (restaurant), 69
Bond, Richard P., 35, 39
Boots Aircraft, 17
Bourke-White, Margaret, 132
Bowman, Lew, 39
Boy Scouts, 41
Braithwaite, E. R., 122
Breslow's store, 61
Breuer, Marcel, 40
Bridgman, Ann, 127, 136
Brinckerhoff, Richard, 6, 25
Brindle, Melbourne, 132
Brinley, D. Putnam, 127
Bristow Bird Sanctuary, 20
Britton, Rebecca, 75
Brooks, Lester, 115, 119, 124
Brooks, Patricia, 10, 67, 71, 119
Brooks, Polly Schoyer, 117
Brooks, Van Wyck, 115
Brotherhood & Higley, 56
Brotherhood, John, 56
Brown, Dr. Charlotte, 43-53
Brown, Dr. David, 5, 43-54
Brown, Rush, 48
Bryant, David, 94
Bryant, Roswell ("Roz"), 19
Bucciarelli family, 26
Bugg, Bob, 134
Bukovcik, John, 136
Burnett, Whit, 121
Burnette, Hallie, 121
Butler, Rev. Richard, 89

Caesar, Harry, 127, 128
Cammerer, Dave, 36
Campbell, David, 75
Campbell, Katie, 75
Campbell, Marge, 25
Canaan Parish, 28
Carriage Barn, 2, 128, 129

Carroll, Ruth, 127, 136
Carroll, Tom, 31
Cassel, John, 134
Catlin, Hoyt, 5
Caulfield, Bob, 26
Caulfield, Jane, 65, 66
Cavelli, Dick, 135
Center School, 18, 26, 75
Chamber of Commerce, 129
Chase Manhattan Bank of Connecticut, 58
Chase, Rev. Loring, 84
Cherida, Inc., 57
Cherry Street East, 68
Ching's Table, 70
Christ-Janer, Albert, 130
Christ-Janer, Victor, 40, 129
Chrostowski, Edmund J., 6, 13, 22, 37, 38, 96
Church of Jesus Christ of Latter-Day Saints, 83, 85
Churchill, Winston, 7
Clausen, Edgar, 17
"Club 31", 62
Coalition for Nuclear Arms Control, 89
Cody Drugstore, 16
Cody, Dr. Thomas P., 4, 24, 31
Cohen, Israel ("Izzy"), 3, 36, 63, 67, 99
Cole, Bruce, 5
Coleman, Harry, 6
Coletto, Joe, 22
Colonial Motors, 58
Colum, Mary, 115
Colum, Padraic, 115
Committee of Common Concern (originally Committee of Christian Concern), 86, 88
Community Baptist Church, 83, 85
Community Foundation, 2
Comstock, Anthony, 6
Congregational Church, 83, 84, 91, 139
Connecticut Bank and Trust Company, 59
Connecticut National Bank, 59
Connecticut Supreme Court, 113
Conner, W. Bidwell ("Pop"), 99
Cooke, Terry, 27

Corner Cigar Store, 62
Corson, Jim, 34
Costales, Clarence E., 16, 47
Cousins, Norman, 119, 132
Cox, Rev. R. David, 89
Crichton, Michael, 120
Cronin, A. J., 120
Cronin, Tom, 99
Cross, Donna Woolfolk, 121
Cunningham, Molly, 25
Curtis, H. Pelham family, 132
CVS (pharmacy), 16

D'Addario firm, 29, 61
Daley, Robert, 122
Dam, Erik, 33, 94
Danes, Gibson, 130
D'Arazien, Art, 135
Dauk, Pete, 101
Davies, E. Kenyon, 63
Davis, Hayward ("Hy"), 97
Delage, George, 28
Deli-Bake, 67
DeMichele quadruplets, 7
Demmerle, Peter, 105
Dickerman's store, 61
DOCOMOMO, 39, 41
Donohue, Mary, 40
Dorne, Albert, 139
Doty, Jean Slaughter, 124
Doty, Roy, 124, 135
Doyle, Joe, 63
Doyle's Tavern, 63
Dumm, Edwina, 134
Dunkin' Donuts, 55
Dunn, Phoebe, 136
Dunn, Susan, 11
Dunning, Jim, 108
DuVal, Philip L. R., 4

Eager, Edward, 122
East School, 75
Eberman, Edwin, 133
Edwards, Douglas, 68
Edwards, Jonathan, 138
Egerman, Mike, 95
Elicker, Gordon, 31
Elise Nursery, 61
Ellington, Duke, 7
Ernst, Jimmy, 127

Erson, Rev. Fredrick E., 89
Esty, Greg, 104
Exchange Club, 23
Exter, Dr. Frederick, 52

Fadiman, Clifton, 117
Fairfield County Trust Company, 58
Fairty farm, 61
Fairty, Charlie, 18
Fairty, Ray, 17
Family Britches, 68
Family Fourth at Waveny, 28
Fat Tuesday, 57, 68
Faus, Jane, 129
Fenick, Vincent, 18, 26
Fenton, Jan, 128
Field Club, 110
Finch, Kip, 14, 18
Finnie, David, 1, 113, 117
First Church of Christ, Scientist, 83, 84, 85
First County Bank, 59
First National (market), 55
First National Bank of New Canaan, 58
First Presbyterian Church, 82, 83, 91
Fischer, Darius, 129
Fitzsimons, John, 31
Fleet Bank, 59
Fleet Boston Financial Corp., 59
Foley, Martha, 116
Ford, Curry E., 6
4-F Striders, 108-109
Four Seasons (farm stand), 18
Four Winds Farm, 18
Franco Family Trust, 57
Franco family, 56
Franco's Wine Merchants, 56, 64
Franzen, Ulrich, 40
French, William, 31
Frothingham, Dr. John, 45

Gates (restaurant), 68, 70
Gelbin, Allan, 40
Geldzheler, Henry, 130
Gibson, Betsy, 42
Gifford, Florence Schick, 131
Gillane's (dry goods), 55
Gilmore, Maurice ("Wilky"), 101-102
Giuliano, Rev. N. P., 85

Index

"Glass House," 40-41, 93
Glazer, Harold, 29
Glidden, A. Leland ("Buddy"), 51-53, 56
Goldberg, Alan, 40
Goldberg, Gertrude Schaffner, 119
Gordon, John, 130
Gores, Landis, 40
Grand Union (supermarket), 15
Green, Gerald, 121
Greenberg, Syd, 75, 136
Gregg, Laicita Worden, 128
Gridiron Club, 2-6, 64
Griffin Ford, 57
Gristede's (grocery), 55
Groher, Julius, 4, 23, 24, 25, 68, 99, 100
Gruelle, Justin, 128, 132
Gruelle, Johnny, 132
Guardian Savings and Loan, 59
Guerrero, Pedro, 135
Gutt, Ed, 5

Hamilton, Helen, 128
Hampton Inn, 56
Hanish, Burt, 17
Harrison, Albert, 132
Hart, William, 29
Hawes, Rodney, 108
Hawthorne, Dana, 25
Haynes, George, 22
Henderson, Tom, 135
Heritage (restaurant), 69
Herman, Bob, 108
Herman, Hamilton, 31
Hersam, John E., 57, 97
Hersam, Jeanne, 57
Hersam, Martin, 57
Hersam, Mary Anne, 57
Hersam, V. Donald, Jr., 57, 67
Herzan, John, 40
Hildebrandt, Howard, 127
Hill, Carlton, 3
Hoagland, Edward, 120
Hobbs, Ted, 22
Hobson, Laura, 122
Hogan, W. Riley, 4
Hokinson, Helen, 135, 137
Holmewood Inn, 55
Horgan, John, 119

Horton, Kurt, 105
Horton, Rick, 105
Houston, I. H. ("Ike"), 51
Howmart Corporation, 29
Hoyt Cinema Corp., 57
Hoyt Farms, 61
Hoyt Funeral Home, 57
Hoyt, Franklin B., 57
Hoyt's Flower Shop, 12, 16
Hoyt's Nursery, 29, 60
Huckleberry's, 70
Huidekooper, Hank, 105
Hunan Taste, 70
Hurricane Gloria, 8

Ice Storm, The, 93-96, 122
Interfaith Service Committee (originally Interchurch Service Committee), 6, 86-87, 88, 91
International Brotherhood of Teamsters, 61
Iovino, Vin, 106
Isselee, Mark, 18
Izzy's Place (see Pierre's)

Jackson's store, 62
Jacobson, Albert, 128
Jake's Modern Barbershop, 17, 56
James, Lem, 105
Janis, Ed, 36, 62
Jeffries, Eve, 42
Johansen, John, 40, 127
Johansen, Mary Ellen, 10
Johnson, David, 133
Johnson, Philip, 8, 40, 41, 69, 93
Jordhamo, Tony, 31

Kammerer, Brian, 132
Karl Buick, 57
Karl Chevrolet, 6, 57
Karl, Emil, 58
Karl, Leo, 58
Karl, Leo, Jr., 6, 58
Karl, Leo, III, 58
Karl, Richard, 58
Keating, Edward, 136
Kelda Group PLC, 56
Keller, Henry ("Red"), 10, 32
Kelley, Charles F., 4, 12, 16-24
Kelley, Mark, 101

Kelley, Roger B., 4
Kennedy, Mary, 122
Keteyian, Armin, 124
Keyes, Loren J., 101
Killiam, Paul, 3, 4, 6, 94, 129
King, Judge, 113
King, Mary Louise, 10, 129
King, Rev. Martin Luther, Jr., 88
Kinne, Russ, 135
Kirby, Walter, 128
Kiwanis Park, 23
Kline, Kevin, 93, 95
Kolodny, Robert and Nancy, 118

La Plume Doree (stationery), 62
L'Abbee (restaurant), 69
Label, Jacques, 108
Labor Day tennis, 110
LaFarge, Henry, 136
Lake Club, 110
Lake, Anthony, 116
Lake, Eleanor, 116
Lamb, Adrian, 127
Lamb, Beatrice Pitney, 117
Lang's Pharmacy, 56, 64
Lapham Community Center, 2, 54
Lapin, Harvey, 66
Lapin, Jean Rosen, 66
Lawson, Katherine, 128
League of Women Voters, 10, 24, 51, 52
Lee, Ang, 93-95
Lee, John Black, 40, 41
Lee, Johnson, 69
Lewis, Chet, 34
Lewis, Torch, 5
Libby's Diner, 69, 71
Liberatore, Gary, 103
Lindner Cycle Shop, 58
Lindstrom, Gary, 40
Lindstrom, Janet, 39, 40, 141
Lions Club, 17
Lipschitz, Jacques, 131
Lisa's Classic Cuts, 56
Lissard House, 69
Little Kitchen of New Canaan, 70
Little Red Schoolhouse, 73
Lloyd, Ruth Lapham, 23
Logan's (restaurant), 69
Lombardo, Nick, 5

~145~

Look magazine, 53
Lorenz, Lee, 135
Lowry, John, 5
Lupica, Mike, 123-124
Lusk, Kay, 52
Lynch, Bob, 104, 105
Lynch, Christopher, 33

Mabel C. Lamb, Inc., 56
MacLane, Jean, 127
Mac's Grill Room, 70
Magic Wok, 70
Maher, John, 103
Maliszewski, Catherine, 67
Malizia, Tony, 101
Mansfield, Walter, 25
Manship, Paul, 127
Maples Inn, 55
Marinelli, Lou, 106
Martin's (store), 69
Matthews, John G., 5, 25
Mattie's (restaurant), 70
Mazzella, Fred, 20
McClelland, John, 130
McConnell, Joyce, 50
McDermott, Dr. Walsh, 52
McKenzie, Malcom, 62
McKenzie's, 62
Mead, Penfield, 5
Mead, Stanley P., 3
Meals on Wheels, 54, 87
Mechanics and Farmers Bank, 58
Meek, Clifton, 128
Melba Inn, 17, 56, 115
Miles, Hank, 129
Miller, Charles P., 15, 26
Miller's Dairy, 61
Milligan, Carina, 28
Mills, Willis N., 74
Mitchell, Ann, 133
Mitchell, Dave, 26
Mitchum, Robert, 68
Modern Plumbing and Heating, 5
Montgomery, Bruce, 31
Montgomery, Marshall, 1, 4
Moody, Rick, 93-95, 122
Moorhead, Thomas, 6
Moreno, Lou, 5, 30, 31, 35, 95
Morrill, Rev. Grant A., 84, 88, 89
Morrow, Tom, 109

Morton, Charles P., 4, 19, 22, 26-30
Mr. Lee (restaurant), 69
Mull, Marty, 109
Mulligan's (restaurant), 69
Murphy, Bill, 102
Murphy, G.C. (store), 55

NAACP, 88
Nantucket Café, 69
National Bank & Trust Co. of Fairfield County, 59
National Trust for Historic Preservation, 8, 40
Nelson, Ralph, 128
New Canaan Advertiser, 3, 6, 8, 11, 57, 68, 88, 94, 96, 97
New Canaan Bank and Trust Company, 59
New Canaan Baseball, Inc., 107
New Canaan Book Shop, 57
New Canaan Cardinals, 98
New Canaan Drug Store, 56
New Canaan Fire Company No. 1, 33
New Canaan Fuel and Lumber Co., 3, 60
New Canaan Grays, 99
New Canaan High School, 30 31, 75, 76, 100-107
New Canaan Historical Society, 2, 8, 13, 14, 39, 56, 78
New Canaan Imported Cars, 58
New Canaan Inn, 2, 42, 54, 87
New Canaan Land Conservation Trust, 2, 10
New Canaan Library, 2, 8, 23, 78, 94
New Canaan Maroons, 98, 99
New Canaan Medical Center, 43
New Canaan Nature Center, 2, 4, 20, 78
New Canaan Neighborhoods, Inc., 28
New Canaan Playhouse, 57
New Canaan Racquet Club, 60, 69
New Canaan Rams, 103-105
New Canaan Redskins, 99, 100
New Canaan Savings Bank, 58
New Canaan Sculpture Group, 128
New Canaan Society for the Arts, 26, 128-129

New Canaan Taxpayers Association, 25
New Canaan Water Company, 8, 51-53, 56
New Canaan Zebras, 64, 99
New England Bancorp, Inc., 58
New York Times, 7-10, 95, 96, 114
Nichols, Gouverneur, 29
Nicklaus, Jack, 7
Nielson, Bob, 5
Noble, Henry S. ("Harry"), 5, 10, 25
Nora Zandre, 56, 64
Norman Dairy, 61
Norwalk Hospital, 34
Noyes, Eliot, 12, 40
Nursing & Home Care, 50-51

Old Faithful Antique Fire Engine Company, 4
O'Neill, Marie, 93
Osborne, Robert, 135
Outback, 2, 89
Outdoor Art Show, 129-131

Packard, Vance, 118
Paggy's (restaurant), 71
Paglialunga, Len, 104-105
Palmer, Dick, 23
Panella, Frank, 105
Partch, Virgil, 135
Peck, Hiram, 39
Pennington, Peil, 104-105
People's Bank, 59
"People's Union", 61
Pereida, Ralph, 6, 23, 133
Perkins, Maxwell, 115, 125
Perrine, Mary, 127
Perrine, Van Dearing, 127
Perry, Lawrence, 103
Person-to-Person, 89
Pickering, John W., 5
Pierre's (restaurant), 36, 62-64, 67, 99
Plum Tree, 70
Poinsettia Club, 53-54
Police Athletic League, 31
Pop Warner football, 107
Powerhouse, 2
Prescott, Ann Lake, 116
Prescott, Orville ("Bill"), 116
Prescott, Peter, 116, 124

Index

Prezzo (restaurant), 70
Prieger, Henry H., 67
Provost, Dan, 26
Putnam Trust, 59

Quinn, Betty, 73-81

Rabe, Ed, 23
Randall, Kathleen, 41
Raymond, Carlton S. ("Pete"), 4, 31, 68, 99
RCA Corporation, 8, 29, 61
Ready, Gene, 101
Redford, Robert, 68
Reiss, Gwen North, 39, 41
Rescue and Restore, 128
Resor, Jane, 49
Resor, Stanley R., 4, 89
Ricco, Darin, 129
Richards, Gary, 31
Richards, Glenora, 127
Richards, Walter DuBois, 11, 72, 127, 139
Rider, Ginny, 128
Rigoletto (restaurant), 70
Risom, Jens, 41
Roger Sherman Inn, 55, 67, 70
Rogers, Henrietta, 6, 24
Rogers, James G., Jr., 5
Rogers, John, 138
Roorbach, William, 122
Roos, Audrey Kelley, 121
Roos, William, 121
Rosen Brothers Market, 55, 65-66
Rosen family, 66
Rosen, Helen, 66
Rosenberg, Jim, 22
Ross, Norman P., 22
Rubin, Steve, 31
Rudolph, Paul, 75
Rutherford, Priscilla, 30
Rutledge, Warren, 99

Saaf, Mike, 19
St. Aloysius Church, 83, 84, 85, 91
St. Claire, E. Kyle, Jr., 89
St. Mark's Episcopal Church, 82, 83, 91
St. Michael's Lutheran Church, 83
Salant Room, 1

Sarnoff, Robert, 29
Sartorio, Rev. Paul L., 89
Saxe Middle School, 75, 93
Saxe, Brock, 17
Saxon, Charles, 17, 126, 135
Schalk, Walter, 138
Schamus, James, 94-95
Schless, Howard, 117
Schlumpf, Jim, 6
Schmidt, Otto, 97
Schmitt, Jake, 99
Schneider, Hans, 22
Schoolhouse Apartments, 4, 5, 27-28, 30, 54, 87
Schundler, Rev. Bruce E., 89
SCM Corporation, 18
Scofield's (furniture), 19, 56
Scott, Ralph M., 33, 101
Seale, Dick, 109
Sears Roebuck, 29, 60
Self, Margaret Cabell, 124
Selinger, Dr. Jerome, 4
Selleck's Corners Chapel, 90
Senior Men's Club, 2, 6, 78
Senior, John L., Jr., 8, 113-114
Sentosa (restaurant), 70
Shawmut National Corp., 59
Shaw's (supermarket), 15
Sickles, Noel ('Bud"), 132
Sikorski, Joseph, 100-106
Silliman's Hardware, 60
Silverberg, Jeroll, 57
Silverberg, Sam, 62
Silvermine College of Art, 131
Silvermine Guild Center for the Arts, 2, 131
Silvermine Market, 57
62 Main Street (restaurant), 69, 70
Sloane, Allan, 121
Smallen, Hugh, 40
Smith, Rev. Charles C., 89
Smith, Earl M., 3, 35, 60
Smith, Earl M., Jr., 60
Smith, Malcolm, 136
Smith, Walter W. ("Red"), 123
Sneakers (restaurant), 70
Soby, James Thrall, 136
Solé Ristorante, 57, 68, 70
Sonsky, Milt, 109
Souden, Don, 6, 97, 111

Souden, Sandy, 109
South Avenue Cottage, 89
South School, 31, 74
Southwest Regional Planning Agency, 22
Speers, Rev. T. Guthrie, Jr., 5, 83, 86, 87-90
Sperry, Armstrong, 123
Spofford Gallery, 64
Stackpole, Steve, 5, 42
Stallone, Sylvester, 68
Stamford Savings Bank, 59
Stang, Arnold, 5
Starbuck's, 55
State National Bank of Connecticut, 59
Sterling, Jack, 4
Stinchfield, Judy, 56
Stoddard, Hudson, 24, 73-81
Stolz, Mary, 123
Stone Horse (restaurant), 70
Stone, Anne, 26
Stone, Edward Durrell, 40
Strays and Others, 2
Strider International, 108-109
Suburban Action Institute, 30
Summit Bank, 59
Sweet, Joseph C., 6, 55, 64, 139
Sweet, Ozzie, 135
Symon, Gail, 131
Szyk, Arthur, 132, 133

Talmadge Hill Community Church, 85
Tamsett, Su, 40
Tandoori Taste of India, 70
Tanner, Ogden, 118
Tarika, Virginia S., 10
Taylor, Rev. Gardner Calvin, 89
Tequila Mocking Bird, 69, 70
Terres, John, 119
Terry, Walter, 117
Thali (restaurant), 70
Thompson Motors, 58
Thoms, Frank, 129
Thornton Fuller (department store), 55
Tiani, Frederick P., 33
Tilley, Herb, 26
Tomaselli, Jim, 105

~147~

Toomey, Bill, 101-102
Toomey, Dick, 102
Toppin, Joe, 24
Totaro's (market), 55
Town band, 6, 139
Town Council, 22, 73
Town Players, 26, 138
Town Restaurant, 68

Union Trust, 58, 70
United Fund, 14
United Methodist Church, 83, 84, 85, 91
United States Supreme Court, 114
United Way, 14
Urban League, 88

Varnum's Pharmacy, 56, 95
Vassos, John, 131
Veterans of Foreign Wars, 35
Vicolo (restaurant), 70
Village Inn, 56
Visiting Nurse Association, 49-51, 54
Volunteer Ambulance Corps, 2, 34, 42, 54

Wakeman, Robert C., 128
Walter Stewart's Market, 55, 65
Walton, Rev. Jon M., 89
Walworth, Nancy Zinsser, 117
Ward, Keith, 132
Washington, Rev. Don A., 89
Waveny Care Center, 2, 6, 23, 42, 43, 54, 87, 89
Waveny estate, 75
Waveny Park, 2, 20
Weaver, Sigourney, 93, 95
Webb, Clifton, 129
Webb, Paul, 134
Weed & Duryea, 60
Weil, Gene, 102
Weilenmann, Thomas and Kay, 67
West School, 31, 75
White Oak Bistro, 69
Whitney Shop, 56
Wilburn, Rev. Gary, 90
Wilkins, Roy, 88
Williams, Mike, 32
Wilser, Dr. Harold, 31, 32
Wilson, Helen Van Pelt, 119

Wilson, Sloan, 122
Winfield, Dick, 5
Winpenny, Edward L., 5
Winter Club, 110
Wood, Lawrence ("Lonnie"), 23
Woolfolk, Joanna, 121
Woolfolk, William, 121
Works Progress Administration (WPA), 128
Woundy, I. B., 12
Wright, Frank Lloyd, 40, 135
Wright, Tom, 5
Wylie, Elinor, 115

Xerox, 61
Y.M.C.A., 2, 6, 31
Yates, Elizabeth, 123
Youmans, Al, 4, 23
Young Women's League, 2, 131
Young, Leslie B., 3, 21, 47
Young, Leslie T., 25
Young, Whitney, 88
Youth Conservation Corps, 28
Zoning Commission, 113
Zumbach's, 55
Zur, Stephen, 67

ILLUSTRATION CREDITS:

William Baldwin Estate: 9
John Bukovcik: 92
Richard Bergmann: 8(middle)125
Nina Bremer: 82 (both), 84 (bottom left & right), 85 (top & bottom)
Patricia Brooks: 67
David Bryant: 95
Alison & Harry Caesar: 128
Tom Casey: 124
Ed Chrostowski: 109
Edwin Eberman: 90
File Illustration/Photo – NCHS: frontpiece, title page, dedication, facing 1, 12, 23, 27, 36, 40, 41, 55, 56 (all), 62, 63, 68, 96, 116, 118 (both),130, 136
Nancy Finnie: 54

Joyce Flaschen: 89
Christopher Frye: drawing below Mission Statement
Syd Greenberg: 3, 5, 21, 42 (bottom), 57, 61, 64, 66, 74, 75, 129, 138 (lower left) (lower right)
Helen Hokinson: 137 ©The New Yorker Collection 1945 Helen Hokinson from cartoonbank.com. All Rights Reserved.
House & Home: 38
Ole Jerrild: 136
Leo Lances Studio: foreword
Lindner: 58 (lower)
Look magazine: 51
New Canaan Advertiser: 12 (lower), 22
Charles P. Miller: 15, 26
Allan Mitchell: back jacket flap
Bernie Nunez: 7
New Canaan Advertiser: 12, 22
Planning & Zoning of New Canaan: 112
Walter DuBois Richards: facing contents, 11, 72, 139 (top), 142
Roger Roth: 9
Charles Saxon: 17, 126
Christine Simmons: 42 (middle)
Alexander Souden: 104
Don Souden: 107
Joseph Sweet: 84 (upper right)
Virgina Taylor: cover
University of Colorado: 102
John Vassos: 131
Waveny Care Center: 42 (top)
Paul Webb: 134

PRODUCTION CREDITS:

Book design and composition: The Casey Group, New Canaan
Text type: Bembo
Printing: Colahan Saunders Corp. Long Island City, NY
Text and jacket paper: Mohawk Superfine
Cover: Arrestox–B
End papers: Fraser's Passport 80 lb.